Money Unbound

MONEY UNBOUND
BITCOIN AND THE BREAKING OF THE OLD WORLD ORDER

Mihir Magudia

Copyright © 2021 Mihir Magudia

All rights reserved.

ISBN: 9798516791338

For Otto Maximilian and Axel Wolfgang.
You two are the reason I'm optimistic about the future.
MM

Table of Contents

Introduction i

1. Noah and Emily Harrison: *Home at Last* 1
2. Amadou Touré: *The High Cost of Poverty* 25
3. Adriana Pereira: *Fighting Crime on New Frontiers* 43
4. Yuri Vasiliyev: *Powering Sustainability* 79
5. Farhan Kazdi: *Escaping the Police State* 96
6. Chaturi Jayartne: *When Opportunity Meets Talent* 117
7. Dwayne Henry: *Money for Peace* 137
   Conclusion 160
   References 169
   About the author 173

Introduction

All the forces in the world are not so powerful as an idea whose time has come.
- VICTOR HUGO

A Brief History of Money

A business maxim states that profit potential is proportional to the problem your business solves. In other words, if you want to make a lot of money, find the biggest problem you can, and solve it. To truly understand the value of cryptocurrency, we have to understand the problem that it fixes, and this requires a quick look at the history of money.

Just about anything can be used as money: we tend to think of money as a physical object when, in reality, it's more of a social construct.

For example, on the island of Yap in the South Pacific in modern-day Micronesia, tribes would even use large stones as money. These so-called *Rai* stones were often too heavy to carry – some weighing up to 2000 kilograms – so when someone made a purchase, the whole tribe simply agreed that ownership of the stone had changed. In some instances, a stone would be lost at sea during transport, but since the tribe agreed the stone must still exist, they continued to use it for buying and selling.

The shells of various marine molluscs, prized as jewellery in parts of Asia, the Americas, Africa, and Australia, were also used by many cultures as a means of exchange; interestingly, the Chinese character for money, 貝, originates from a drawing of a cowry shell.

It became clear very early on, however, that good money should be *scarce*. Shell-based monetary systems often ran into trouble as clever individuals found abundant sources of shells and brought them in from farther afield, devaluing the currency and disrupting economies.

Gold and silver proved more resistant, but not immune, to this phenomenon. Mansa Musa, a wealthy African king, famously lavished gifts of gold on a visit to the Middle East in the 13th century, leading to the devaluation of gold and major disruptions to the local economies of Egypt and Arabia. Likewise, after the conquest of the Americas, the Spanish conquistadors brought so much gold and silver to Europe that the value of the currency crashed, causing economic chaos.

Another problem with gold and silver was the potential for faking or diluting the value of the coins. In Imperial Rome, the infamous and insane Emperor Nero began to debase the *denarius*, a silver coin that served as the empire's currency. By mixing small quantities of less valuable metals with the silver, it was possible to pay the salaries of soldiers and public servants while reducing the overall expense to the state.

Nero is one of the best examples of how wrong things can go when the power to issue currency is put in the hands of evil individuals. After a devastating fire in Rome, instead of rebuilding the city and providing assistance to the victims, Nero made matters worse by using the profits from degrading the currency to construct a lavish pleasure palace. The palace included features like a 37-metre-tall statue of Nero himself and a mechanism that showered rose petals from the ceiling during the nightly feasts and orgies.

As if this state of affairs wasn't bad enough, the introduction of paper money made it even easier to devalue currencies and indirectly steal wealth from the people who were using them. This system was introduced in Europe a few centuries later.

In 1668, a man named Johan Palmstruch founded the *Riksbank* in Sweden: a grand experiment that was to become Europe's first central bank. At the time, Sweden used large copper plates called *dalers* as its currency. These *dalers* could sometimes weigh as much as 20 kilograms, which was not very convenient when doing the shopping. The Swedish crown was also heavily in debt at the time, so when Palmstruch approached the government with a plan to stimulate the economy, they happily granted him permission to issue paper money.

The system proved relatively popular. The people could use handy pieces of paper for buying and selling rather than the cumbersome *dalers*. Everything was going just fine until the government decided to start issuing new *dalers* that weighed 17 per cent less than the old ones. This meant that the value of older *dalers* went up relative to the newer ones, and depositors appeared at the Riksbank demanding their old *dalers* back. Mr Palmstruch, however, didn't have the people's money because he'd been loaning it out at interest.

So Palmstruch hatched what must have seemed like a brilliant plan at the time. Instead of returning the *dalers*, he just offered more paper proofs of deposit. This worked for a time, but with the influx of paper money on the market, the value of the Riksbank notes eventually collapsed. Businesses suddenly had no access to funds, and a deep recession struck Sweden.

The people were understandably upset, and soon enough, Palmstruch found himself before a tribunal, which sentenced him to death for his crimes. Mr Palmstruch was later pardoned, but the Riksbank lives on and still issues the Swedish krone today.

While adding lower value metals to coins made it possible for the government to steal from the salaries of public servants, the advent of paper money enabled central bankers to steal from everyone. Creating new currency will gradually lower the value of the currency overall, transferring wealth from the holders of the old money to holders of the newly created money. But this begs the question: if paper money is so bad, why did anyone accept it in the first place?

The earliest mention of paper currency comes from Imperial China. In the 13th century, Marco Polo was the first European known to have witnessed the use of paper money during his travels to China. When he recounted his story back in Europe, his amazed listeners asked why anyone would accept paper as a form of payment. The answer was simple: if you refused, the emperor would kill you.

Again and again, throughout history, the management of money has fallen into the hands of irresponsible, incapable, and sometimes outright evil individuals. The results were similar every time: savings destroyed, economies in depression, and mass unemployment. In many cases, these crises even lead to horrific wars. The collapse of the *mark*, the currency of Weimar Germany in the run-up to World War II, is one of the most well-known examples.

Too Big to Fail?

Eighty-five million people dying, with hyperinflation playing a major role, seems pretty bad, doesn't it? But wait! It gets even worse. For most of the 20th century, the value of national currencies was tied to gold. Just as in the story of Mr Palmstruch, you could go to a bank at any time and exchange your paper for a physical commodity – usually gold.

The financial meltdown that contributed to Hitler's rise to power resulted, in part, from the suspension of this arrangement. The German government chose to end the mark's convertibility to gold in order to pay the reparations debt from the First World War.

So you must be thinking, if that was such an awful decision, surely no one would ever, ever do it again, right? Actually, after the end of the Second World War, world leaders decided to implement a worldwide gold standard. The international financial system would be based on the United States dollar, they agreed, and the dollar would be convertible to gold. So far, so good.

This didn't last for long, though. With the advent of the Vietnam War, the United States began quietly expanding the supply of dollars to finance the war effort. Soon, France began to doubt America's ability to honour its obligations and asked for gold instead of paper. Recalling once again the case of Mr Palmstruch, the French were informed that America didn't have enough gold to cover its obligations. But, unlike Mr Palmstruch, America had the most powerful military in the world, so instead of being thrown in prison and sentenced to death, the Americans announced an end to the gold standard and thus began an era of unlimited money printing that continues to this day.

This decision made the same mistake as that of Weimar Germany, but this time it affected the entire world rather than just one country.

The money supply steadily expanded, and purchasing power steadily declined. Since the inflation rate was relatively low, this arrangement seemed to work alright for a while. Cracks began to appear, however, in 2007 with the subprime mortgage crisis, which spiralled into a global financial crisis.

Since the banks could create money at will, they weren't too careful when handing out loans. After all, the more they lent, the more interest they'd receive, so *the more, the merrier*, they thought. But their balance sheets gradually swelled with toxic loans from under-qualified borrowers. Soon, a number of banks found themselves insolvent and facing total collapse.

Banks around the world were heavily invested in American financial markets, so the crisis quickly reached global proportions. As the shock hit the markets, trillions of dollars' worth of wealth was completely wiped out. Rather than leave the irresponsible banks to their much-deserved fate, the central banks of the world stepped in to buy up the bad debt.

In the five years following the outbreak of the crisis, the United States Federal Reserve created over four trillion dollars in new money to bail out distressed banks, claiming they were "too big to fail". The Bank of England followed suit, creating over 400 billion pounds the European Central Bank created over two trillion, and the Bank of Japan nearly three trillion.

Of course, they didn't say that they were creating vast sums of money out of nothing. Instead, they called it quantitative easing. Sounds soothing somehow, doesn't it? The reality is not so benign, however. Given the past history of episodes of unlimited monetary expansion, many observers found this massive expansion of the money supply very worrying. All hope was not lost – the search for a better money was already underway.

The Quest for Digital Gold

The problems associated with metal and paper currency are well understood, and almost as soon as the internet was born, the search for electronic cash began. Nobel Prize-winning Economist Milton Friedman predicted the significance that such an invention would have, saying:

> *I think that the internet is going to be one of the major forces for reducing the role of government. The one thing that's missing, but that will soon be developed, is a reliable e-cash, a method whereby on the internet you can transfer funds from A to B without A knowing B or B knowing A.*

In 1983, David Chaum proposed an idea for e-cash, an anonymous electronic cash. He was later able to partner with one bank to implement it, but the project fizzled out rather quickly. Chaum's e-cash was simply a means of anonymously transferring ordinary dollars. What was really needed was a better currency.

E-gold, a popular gold-backed currency founded in 1996, was one such attempt. The idea was simple: a company held a vault of gold and issued digital certificates which were redeemable for gold. It saw rapid growth after 2000, but as it grew, it came under increasing legal pressure from regulators. Finally, in 2007, it was shut down amid a complex legal controversy.

The Liberty Dollar was another attempt to create an alternative, gold-backed currency. Conceived as a privately issued currency by a group of American Libertarians, it met a more dramatic end when the FBI raided the office of its founder, Bernard von Nothaus, and seized all of the gold reserves. Nothaus was arrested and threatened with a 23-year prison sentence for making, possessing and selling his own coins.

It might seem strange that making your own coins would be punished more severely than rape or armed robbery, but the authorities insisted that Nothaus was guilty of a "unique form of domestic terrorism". Nothaus spent several years in prison before his sentence was finally reduced to six months' house arrest and three years' probation.

Digital money seems like a natural evolutionary step, but it's actually quite understandable why the authorities would not allow it. Imagine if you had a money printing machine and could print as much money as you liked. Sounds good, doesn't it? If you did, you probably wouldn't want anyone coming along and breaking your monopoly.

Ultimately, it was an online message group calling themselves cypherpunks that finally proposed the solution to the digital currency conundrum. The cypherpunks are a group of activists united by a belief in the potential of cryptography to tackle social problems, including government overreach. Much of their work centres on developing encrypted messaging techniques to help circumvent censorship by totalitarian regimes. Most of the participants share a strong belief in the value of freedom of speech and the potential of technology to defend it.

The freedom of money and freedom of speech are actually quite closely connected if you think about it. After all, today, most of the money in the world is simply information on bank computers. When you transfer money to another account, the transaction is nothing more than a signal in a database that changes a number in your account and adjusts the number in someone else's account – an exchange of information, not unlike the transfer of *Rai* stones.

So in this day and age, financial transactions are essentially a form of communication rather than a physical trade. So why should the freedom to transact be regarded as any different than the freedom to speak?

Cypherpunks view the rights of individuals as a bulwark against the abuses that become possible when power becomes too concentrated. As the saying goes, power corrupts, and absolute power corrupts absolutely. In the cypherpunks' view, government control over what currency individuals use to transact, and how they transact, constitutes a form of oppression.

It was this community that first proposed Bitcoin.

Bitcoin was a radical proposal to establish something that had never existed before – *digital scarcity*. The internet disrupted many business models because it was so easy to copy information. In particular, the publishing and music industries struggled to adapt to the new reality. Bitcoin leveraged cryptographic technology to generate a currency that was digital but whose quantity was fixed. The ability to create a digital good that *cannot be copied* at will may be remembered as a defining moment in the history of the internet and the history of money.

However, the most important thing about Bitcoin was that it used cryptography to delegate the power of money creation to a peer-to-peer network, which ensured that no government could shut that network down.

The invention of Bitcoin was directly inspired by the problems with other forms of money. Bitcoin's mysterious and pseudonymous inventor, Satoshi Nakamoto, wrote:

The root problem with conventional currency is all the trust that's required to make it work. The central bank must be trusted not to debase the currency, but the history of fiat currencies is full of breaches of that trust. Banks must be trusted to hold our money and transfer it electronically, but they lend it out in waves of credit bubbles with barely a fraction in reserve.

Nakamoto's concerns are every bit as valid now as they were when Bitcoin was first developed. In the immediate aftermath of the 2008 crisis, it seemed like things might get better. Public outrage about the excesses of bankers was at an all-time high, and legislation was drafted to increase reserve requirements.

Unfortunately, it seems that things have not gotten better, however. In fact, the situation has gotten worse.

COVID: Failing to Learn the Lessons of the Past

Winston Churchill once said, "Those who fail to learn from history are doomed to repeat it." History is filled with tragedies resulting from the unrestrained creation of money, and yet somehow, we still haven't learned our lesson.

In the 2008 financial crisis, trillions of dollars were created out of nothing and pumped into the global economy. Many will argue that now, things are somehow different, and the banking system can create as much as it wants without any adverse consequences. Defenders of the central banking system like to point to consumer inflation rates. The price of bread and milk are increasing by only two per cent a year, they say, despite the huge quantities of money being created.

This ignores the fact that much of this newly created money is going towards home loans, pushing up property prices, which are not included in standard measures of inflation. This is partly to blame for sky-high rents and property prices. Young people today have a much harder time buying a home than their parents or grandparents did, and in terms of purchasing power, the wages of workers have declined significantly over the last 30 years, while extravagant bonuses for bankers have grown bigger and bigger.

Initially, higher home prices might appear to boost the economy because they drive the construction sector and generate jobs. In the long run, however, this generates unsustainable amounts of debt, and all of the newly created money flooding the markets sends false signals to builders and investors, leading to the formation of a housing bubble. When the bubble bursts, people are unable to make good on their debts, resulting in a downward spiral of defaults and unemployment.

The fact that the creation of so much new money in the 2008 financial crisis did *not* result in hyperinflation seems to have emboldened central banks even more. With the onset of the 2020

COVID pandemic, governments and central banks appear to be treating the ability to create money as an elixir that can cure all ills.

In response to the economic effects of lockdowns, central banks across the world began pumping billions of dollars of so-called *helicopter money* into economies in the shape of stimulus checks and other forms of financial support. In the months following the beginning of COVID lockdowns, the US Federal Reserve Bank of the United States (the Fed) created over $4 trillion – approximately the same amount of money created in the ten years following the 2008 financial crisis.

It seems that the banking system thinks of itself as being so big that it can't possibly fail. It's hard to argue with this because, in terms of monetary policy, we are in completely uncharted territory. The amounts of money being created are unprecedented, so there is no data available to predict exactly what will happen.

The hyperinflation that Germany faced in the run-up to World War II accounted for a relatively small percentage of the world economy. Now, we are facing a massive expansion of the money supply on a global scale. This is a much larger economy, so naturally, it can absorb a much bigger shock.

However, history has been quite consistent. Whenever the ruling authorities begin to create money at will, bad things happen. Expert economists have mixed views on current policies: some dismiss the threat of inflation, while others make ominous prophecies. In the end, common sense would seem to dictate that you cannot simply create as much money as you want and face no consequences.

This situation is nothing more or less than a severe addiction to debt and easy money. It's a bit like an alcoholic who, after a heavy night of drinking, wakes up with a throbbing headache and decides to dull the pain by having another drink.

We no longer have to accept the status quo and become victims of the failure to learn the lessons of history. Bitcoin is more than just digital cash – it's the beginning of a new financial system that is powerfully insulated from the possibility of human error.

Can't Do Evil

Bitcoin is revolutionary because it is the first currency in history issued without the control of any central authority. Bitcoin advocate Andreas Antonopoulos termed this approach *Can't Do Evil*. For many, Bitcoin represents the separation of money and state by completely removing the power of human hands to manipulate the currency.

Although you may find this difficult to understand at first, don't worry! It's quite normal to be bewildered by cryptocurrency, especially when you're just starting out. There's a lot of information to digest, and much of it is quite technical. Many books on Bitcoin and cryptocurrency attempt to introduce the reader to blockchain technology and its applications, but it's not all that important to understand exactly how Bitcoin works. After all, you don't *really* understand *how* your mobile phone works, do you? Neither do I. And yet, we all use them and recognise that they have changed our lives in very powerful ways.

The technological breakthrough represented by cryptocurrency is certainly a marvel, but the true value of the technology lies in its power to transform our lives. This book covers all the basics that beginners need to know to get up to speed with the world of cryptocurrency. It's also about much more than understanding the technology; it's about exploring the human dimension and the transformative impact the technology can have on the lives of real people. Each chapter begins with a story about fictional yet very real characters whose lives are deeply affected by cryptocurrency.

We use these stories as a starting point for examining important topics concerning cryptocurrency and other critical issues of our time, including the environment, crime, immigration, and geopolitics. Like cryptocurrency, these topics are very broad, incredibly complex, and often seem removed from our everyday lives, so why should we even care? Well, because looking at the ways that ordinary people can benefit from the technology helps us to connect these abstract topics to concrete, human realities.

I hope this approach will inspire the reader with enthusiasm for the peaceful revolution that is currently underway. Whether you already know a lot about cryptocurrency or you're a complete beginner, this book has something to offer.

The stories we tell here also illustrate the ways in which our present financial system causes pain and suffering to millions of people – from illegal immigrants, risking their lives at sea in search of a better chance in life; to impoverished slum dwellers, struggling to make ends meet, the world needs borderless opportunities now more than ever. We cannot accept that millions of innocent people should lose their life savings due to the incompetence or malevolence of a few corrupt elites. We now have the power to do something about this state of affairs, and we must act.

Cryptocurrency is an idea whose time has come. There is no turning back the change that's upon us. Like any technology, it can be used for good or evil. We cannot sit back and passively let this change happen. We must be proactive about shaping a new financial order that serves the interests of humanity rather than exploiting the majority for the benefit of a tiny few.

This book is intended to help move us towards a collective vision of the kind of future we want to live in. Although Bitcoin, blockchain, and the cryptocurrency ecosystem are now bigger than most of us ever imagined, we are still at the beginning of this transformation. It's not too late to participate, and there are both moral and financial reasons to do so.

I sincerely hope that this book motivates readers to take an active role in building a new financial order that will enable a better future for humanity. It may seem bold to speak about the future when we live in such uncertain times, but it is precisely in times of uncertainty that we most need an optimistic vision of the future. Such a vision can be a source of hope – and this hope is essential if we are going to make it through these difficult times.

1. Noah and Emily Harrison

Home at Last

Noah and Emily Harrison were an average English working-class couple who never imagined they'd become homeowners. Their parents had always rented; they rented, and that seemed to be the order of things. So a major financial crisis was the last thing they would have expected to propel them into homeownership. But life rarely turns out as we expect.

Emily and her husband, Noah, had always dreamed of owning a home of their own, but they lived in the London borough of Croydon, where house prices were way beyond their reach. Anyway, renting wasn't so bad, so there was no real need to struggle to buy a house. At least, that's the way it seemed. One day, however, when Emily was six months pregnant with the couple's first child, their landlord rang and announced that he'd sold their building to a property developer.

The building was going to be demolished to make way for a luxury high-rise. A month later, the new owner gave them notice – they had two months to find a new home. Ordinarily, this wouldn't have been a major catastrophe, but with the baby on the way, things couldn't possibly have been worse.

With help from their recently retired parents, the move went relatively smoothly, although it was still quite stressful. But barely a year later, as their son, Oliver, was taking his first steps in the new flat, they received the same notice again. Their building had been sold.

Eventually, after months of anxious waiting, a letter arrived announcing that the new owner would renew their rental contract. Despite the reassuring news, the uncertainty was getting too much for them. They were ready for a change. They wanted a sense of security in London's rapidly changing urban landscape.

The couple longed to raise their son in a more stable home, but they couldn't possibly get financing with Noah's salary. Then the global financial crisis struck, and their dream slipped even further out of reach.

Debt spun out of control, and the financial sector suffered a wave of defaults, hitting the world economy hard. As credit lines dried up, factories were forced to shut their doors, and supply chain shocks caused a domino effect. The value of foreign exchange markets collapsed as investors rushed to protect their wealth.

Noah's hours were cut back severely, but the couple were happy to have any work at all. Many of their friends were not so lucky. Since everyone had less money, a credit crunch set in, and housing prices collapsed. Ironically, property was at its most affordable in years, and yet very few had the money to buy, Emily and Noah included.

Emily was working part-time as a shop assistant, and with their combined income, the family could barely make ends meet. They had no choice but to move in with Emily's parents.

This made Noah's commute to work considerably longer, and now they were four adults and one small child cramped into a two-bedroom flat with one toilet. The stress of the commute, the financial difficulties, and the challenges of sharing the small space would occasionally cause tempers to flare. On the bright side, Emily's parents were happy to help look after little Oliver, but when Emily learned she was pregnant with their second child, they all understood the situation was not sustainable.

And yet, they saw no way out. Difficult as it was, it got worse. Banks began imposing withdrawal limits to avoid collapse. And people soon realised the money they'd thought was safe in their account was not there at all. Rioters demanding their savings clashed with police in the streets. Emily and Noah preferred to stay as far away from the protests as possible – they just wanted to take care of their children.

Although rather quiet and not particularly political, they were a social couple and managed to stay busy during the crisis. Any excuse to get out of the cramped house was welcome, and since they'd grown up in the area, they had many friends nearby.

To help make ends meet, they began keeping chickens in the small garden of Emily's parents' terraced house. Many of their friends could no longer afford nursery for their children, so while Noah was at work, Emily would visit friends and help them with the children. None of them had any money to pay her, so in exchange, they would help out however they could. Some of them were unemployed mechanics, so they'd volunteer their maintenance services. Others would offer clothing for Oliver that their kids had outgrown. Others shared homemade preserves.

The debates in parliament went on, and on, and on. It seemed there was no end in sight to the crisis. Emily, Noah and Oliver continued living from day to day. Oliver's little sister, Lisa, came along, and the small house became even more cramped.

Times were lean, but they scrimped and saved and learned to share, and their lives actually became richer through the crisis. Not only had they deepened their relationships with their friends, but they'd also got to know many of their neighbours. Noah was quite a skilled handyman, and his skills were in much demand in the neighbourhood. Although hardly anyone could afford to pay him anything, he never ran short of mince pies and built up a lot of goodwill.

One day, Noah and Emily were out walking with Oliver and baby Lisa in the buggy on their way to help some friends who had a cracked radiator that needed replacing, when they ran into their old friend Vincent. He was very excited and hardly let them say hello before he was enthusing about a new scheme.

"It's a community financing scheme based on social credit. It works with some kind of AI-driven algorithm, and you can use it to get financing." Despite Vincent's excitement, both Noah and Emily were sceptical. They'd heard too many horror stories about investment schemes.

"That's very kind of you, Vincent," said Noah, "but really, we have no cash to spare."

"That's the beauty of it, don't you see? You don't have to pay anything. It's based on your social network."

When they realised he wasn't asking for money, their interest was piqued, and they listened closer.

"Ah! I see. But what am I supposed to get out of it? I mean, there's no such thing as a free lunch, right?"

Vincent continued, "Well, you seem to get on pretty well with everyone in the neighbourhood. You can get credit based on your reputation. And you can start a crowdfund to get financing. If you get enough local people involved, you can attract investors from all over the world."

Emily's face lit up, "So you think we could use this to get our own place?" she asked.

"I just used it to get a motorcycle for my delivery business, but you know loads more people than I do."

"But even if we could get a loan, it's not like we could actually pay it back." Noah objected.

"That's the best part," said Vincent. "There are also internal network credits, so anyone who helps you with financing can also agree to give you credits for your labour."

"But what happens," said Emily, "if people just take the money and run?"

"Well, that's the thing. It has collateral just like a traditional bank loan, but the collateral can be provided by a number of people. Everyone in the neighbourhood trusts you, so you'd probably have no trouble collecting enough pledges to get financing."

Vincent went on to explain that the idea, originally called a *local exchange trading system*, came with an app that community members used to keep track of the goods and services they exchanged. But with the growing popularity of cryptocurrency, multiple local exchange networks had now connected to become a worldwide phenomenon.

Many of Emily and Noah's friends shared their predicament – they had the skills and were willing to work, but there was no money anywhere. So the idea was gaining ground: help out your friends and neighbours, get help in exchange, and access to an international pool of finance. The credits inside the exchange were a form of currency in themselves. You could work and then exchange the credits you earned for the goods and services offered by other members.

Emily and Noah didn't understand exactly how it worked, but Vincent's excitement was infectious. They thanked him and resolved to download the app as soon as they got home.

With the app downloaded, they created a funding profile describing their situation. They sent out invitations to some of their best friends, who also downloaded the app and made collateral pledges. Word spread quickly, and soon all of the goodwill they'd been spreading turned into hundreds of supporters. Some countries were handling the crisis better than others. For many small scale international investors searching for good investments, social credit analysis algorithms were one of the few promising areas in an otherwise bleak investment climate.

With such a large pool of investors to draw upon and with plenty of social data reinforcing their creditworthiness, the funds began to pour in. Some investors contributed as little as £5, while the largest contribution was £5,000. Their parents sold some of their old gold jewellery and contributed £2,000. All in all, almost six thousand investors from some 80 countries contributed over £300,000.

Soon, the funds were released, and they were able to move into their own two-bedroom terraced house not far from Emily's parents. They continued to help and support their friends and neighbours, and in exchange, their friends and neighbours made small contributions to paying off the loan. In a given month, 30 or 40 of their relatives, friends, and neighbours might make payments amounting to around £30 each, but all told, this came to around a thousand pounds. Noah and Emily were also able to contribute a few hundred pounds a month from Noah's salary.

In exchange for their support, friends of the Harrison family received time credits which they could exchange for babysitting and handyman services from the very grateful young family.

Finally, the economy began to improve, and Noah went back to working full-time. The payments made by their support circle gradually decreased as they were able to carry the weight of the loan themselves – having bought their house during the crisis, they'd acquired it at a bargain price.

Noah's boss finally asked him to come back to full-time working, but he and Emily found that they missed the socialising and sense of community they had in the social credit scheme. They realised that they were already making a decent living serving their community, so Noah decided to quit his job. They began working more and more for time credits from their friends and neighbours and were able to help some of their friends purchase homes as well.

Gradually, people began to understand that the money they'd lost to the banks didn't actually exist. It just represented the willingness of people to work on each other's behalf. And more than just being able to realise the dream of homeownership, by leveraging the goodwill derived from their service to their community, the Harrisons were able to achieve financial independence.

All it took for them to achieve their dreams was a system capable of recognising that value. Looking back, they saw the financial crisis as the best thing that had ever happened to them.

✳ ✳ ✳

When Finance Becomes a Barrier to Productivity

Money is basically a representation of the productive power of society. When a financial crisis hits, there's a shortage of money, which can result in unemployment. This unemployment might be due to financial distortion, even if there are no other reasons for work to grind to a halt. While finance can enhance productivity at times, at other times, it can stop it.

For example, consider the case of Argentina, whose currency has collapsed from inflation multiple times in recent history. One such instance of hyperinflation hit Argentina hard in 2001. Savings were wiped out, and a number of companies went bankrupt. The senior management of some factories had the unenviable task of explaining to all the workers that they no longer had jobs. And so, the workers went home, probably feeling a bit depressed.

But at some point, someone realised the factory was just sitting there, empty. There were no other jobs available, so some of the workers had the idea of breaking in and starting to work. They formed an organisation to manage the factory and market the products themselves. The workers were able to keep working, and there was still demand for the products, so why should they stop working just because the bank forced the owner of the factory to shut down? Factories are still operating today under the very same model.

Austria has a similar story from the Great Depression of the 1930s. A wave of unemployment was afflicting Europe, and the resulting lack of cash had frozen up the economy in the Austrian village of Worgl, so the locals decided to create a currency of their own. To encourage spending, they designed it to lose value at a fixed rate. Miraculously, the unemployment level in the village sank from around 40 per cent to close to zero.

Of course, the National Bank of Austria saw this as a threat to its authority and quickly shut the experiment down, but not before it had illustrated a point: if given the freedom to manage their own affairs, communities are capable of organising their productive capacity efficiently.

In the past, experiments like Worgl have worked on a very small scale. Harnessing the power of finance on a large scale has been the job of the banking system. This is not because alternative systems don't work, as the story of Worgl shows. Rather, it's because political pressure would not allow them to work.

With advances in technology, however, the legacy banking system is rapidly losing its grip.

With cryptocurrency, we no longer need a guardian for our account balances. As for finding worthy investments, in many cases, machine learning algorithms are already outperforming traditional loan underwriters. And Bitcoin also solved the problem of requiring a trusted third party for money transfers and the need for a central bank to manage the issuance of currency.

Let that sink in. Bitcoin gives us the means to maintain secure bank accounts and make secure money transfers and issue currency without the need to trust a bank. We can save money and send and receive money anywhere in the world without any need for a bank. Furthermore, we can send fractions of a penny or billions of pounds instantly and securely – there are no more minimums or maximums on money transfers.

This may seem like a small difference, but the possibilities opened up by the increased mobility of digital money are tremendous. Combined with machine learning, this will render the old financial paradigm obsolete, very much in the way that email and text messaging have diminished the role of the paper mail.

Breaking Down Banking

It's not difficult to understand the main problems with fiat currency. When governments try to solve their problems by creating money out of thin air, the currency loses its value due to increased supply relative to demand. Fiat currency is not just a type of money — it's one piece of a larger system.

Today, when you deposit money in a bank, the money no longer legally belongs to you. It becomes the property of the bank to use as they see fit. In exchange, you get a deposit account, which is a liability on the bank's balance sheet. In other words, every time you deposit money in your bank account, you are making a loan to the bank.

We've come to think of this as normal, but it's really rather strange. In short, this just means that banks hold a small percentage of their total liabilities in the form of ready cash, usually just enough to cover demand from depositors.

Let's break down what this means for us today. We can imagine the banking system like a box: money goes in, in the form of deposits, and comes out in the form of loans.

The present model might look something like this:

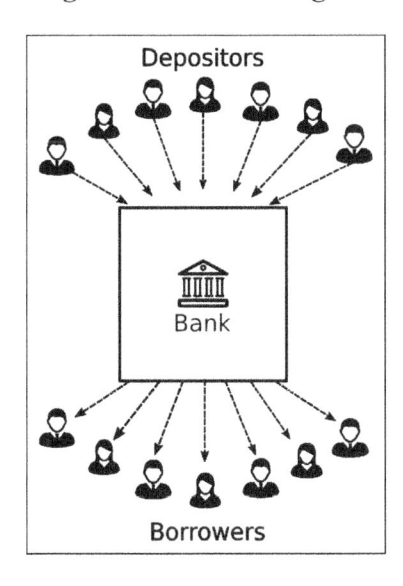

But this is a "magical" box because much more money comes out than ever goes in. Well, actually, for the most part, the money doesn't come out at all. It's just added to the bank accounts of the borrowers. Most money on bank balance sheets never exists outside their balance sheet. So in a way, this is a magical illusion box that makes us feel as if there is far more money than there actually is. And this illusion depends on everyone keeping their money in the bank.

This system has some advantages – it leads to more economic activity because people make many purchases that they can't actually afford. On the other hand, it also inflates asset prices to dangerous levels, fuelling speculative bubbles and leading to unsustainable levels of debt. In Emily's case, we talked about a very real expression of this problem that many young people in the UK face – sky-high property values making homeownership all but impossible.

This highlights a vicious cycle that works out in favour of banks. With so much magical money floating around, speculators buy up properties, driving up property prices. With so many buyers in the market, prices go up. And up. And up. Until almost no one can actually afford a house anymore, except for the people who are already rich and have endless credit lines with the banks.

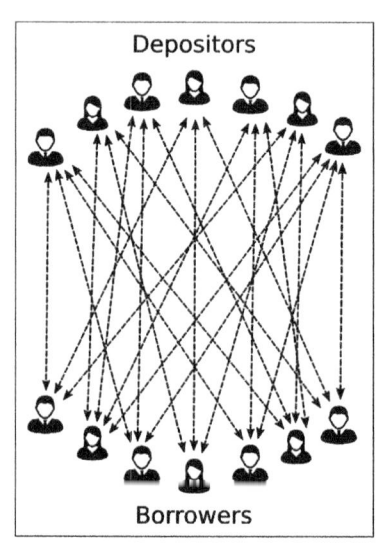

This situation is especially severe in London because this artificial money is being created worldwide. International investors are flooding London with money, driving up housing prices to absurd levels, which has left millennials in a difficult spot. Millennials today spend nearly a quarter of their total income on housing. This is more than triple what the pre-World War II generation paid. Even in the 1980s, it took the average Briton three years to save enough money for a down payment on a house. Today, it takes 19 years.

London-based journalist Michael Goldfarb has this to say about the situation:

> *It will take an epochal catastrophe – like the great depression followed by a war – to allow ordinary people to get into the housing market.*

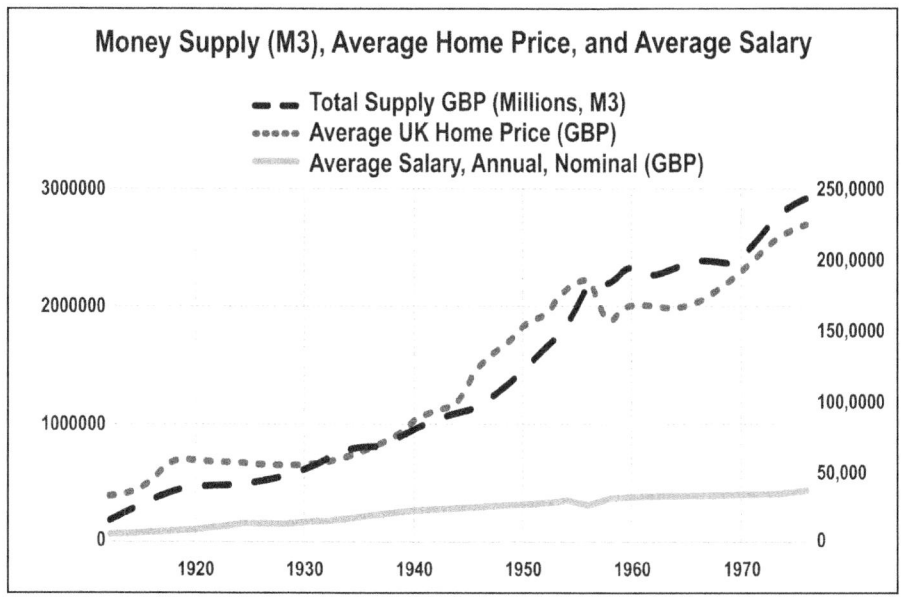

Money Supply (M3), Average Home Price, and Average Salary

- - Total Supply GBP (Millions, M3)
····· Average UK Home Price (GBP)
── Average Salary, Annual, Nominal (GBP)

Chisholm, Kirk. A Visual History of Income Inequality in the US. Wall Street Wisdom. March 5, 2015.

The situation in the United States is very similar. In 1940, a worker earning the minimum wage in the US earned 21% of the price of an average house in one year. Today, the annual minimum wage is less than 6% of the value of a house.

This endless cycle of money creation and debt is problematic beyond just driving up the cost of buying a home. In the long run, this excessive debt becomes a problem for everyone, even those of us who have no interest in owning a home. When debt levels grow too high, if anything disrupts the economy, it can lead to a cascade of defaults with terrible consequences, not the least of which is banks running out of money. If the banks go bankrupt, the economy, which is now completely addicted to debt, grinds to a halt. The International Monetary Fund has cited global debt levels as a major threat to the global economy.

Both of the solutions to the debt crisis involve stealing money from ordinary people. When debt levels become too high, governments have two options:

- Take more money from taxpayers in the form of taxes.
- Create more money out of nothing, which is a way of taking money from the people in the form of inflation.

We're told we have to accept this situation because we couldn't possibly live without banks.

But what would happen if we simply allowed the banks to die as a result of their own foolishness? Would we really all starve to death without the banks organising loans to farmers to purchase their equipment?

Let's suppose we were to lift up the box that represented the bank in the last image and see what's happening underneath. We would see that the bank is mediating a vast, interconnected network of credits, debits, and exchanges. This network might look something like this:

The real value of the economy is in the goods and services that are exchanged. The bank is just responsible for keeping track of this value, and they create money out of nothing in order to do so.

It looks a bit messier than the centralised version. Organising all this to maximise productivity might very well be hard work. But is it hard enough for us to forgive bankers for creating massive bonuses for themselves at everyone else's expense? Perhaps – if we needed them. But with the invention of Bitcoin, we don't anymore.

Previously, we needed experts to maintain the integrity of complex bank ledgers and all of the account balances. We also needed them to safeguard the entries in those ledgers. We also needed them to confirm our account balance and keep track of our personal finances. And of course, we still need banks for making transfers, whether by cheque or other methods.

Bitcoin accomplishes all of this without the need to trust anyone.

But how exactly did Bitcoin achieve this? There's a lot of fuss about blockchain, but the blockchain is actually only one of several mechanisms needed to make the network work. Four core technologies work together to make an open financial system possible: cryptography, blockchain, proof-of-work, and peer-to-peer networks.

Bitcoin and Blockchain Explained

Cryptography

Cryptography is the most important element of Bitcoin – hence the term *cryptocurrency*. Cryptography is defined as the art of writing or solving codes. It is generally applied to encoding and decoding communications so that they can only be read by the intended recipient and no one else.

It's long been understood that cryptography could have powerful applications. In the early days of the internet, the United States government tried to classify the algorithms which Bitcoin is based on as weapons-grade technology which could only be used by military personnel. This stance was overturned in a court battle in the US, where the right of civilians to use high-grade cryptographic codes was upheld on the basis of freedom of speech.

The type of cryptography most important to Bitcoin and foundational to the entire field of cryptocurrency is called *public-key cryptography*.

You may have played with codes as a child. A simple code, for example, would be something like this: A=1, B=2, C=3, and so on. So if you wanted to write "Hello" in a secret message to your friend, you would write 8-5-12-12-15. In this case, your *key* is the document that tells you that A=1, B=2, and so on.

Public-key cryptography is quite a bit more complex, but the important thing to understand is that it uses two keys instead of one. One key is public, and the other private. The public key is used to encrypt the data, but only the holder of the private key can decrypt it. With Bitcoin, the public key functions as an address, not unlike an email address. The private key works as a password.

With public-key cryptography, anyone can use a public key to verify that a signature made by a private key is authentic without actually knowing the private key. With Bitcoin, this allows the network to verify that a transaction is authentic. This is important because Bitcoin has *no central authority* to verify that your password (private key) is correct. Everyone in the world must be able to see that you know your password, but obviously, you can't give everyone in the world your password. Cryptography enables everyone to know that you know your password without you giving it to them.

Cryptography on its own was not enough to create real digital money, however. Even if you could use cryptography to ensure the security of the data, you could not ensure the *scarcity* of the data because anyone could just change their account balance to give themselves more money. To send money, you have to modify your account balance, but if you could modify it however you wanted, you could send more money than you actually have.

This is ultimately why, before Bitcoin, all attempts at digital currency failed. Satoshi Nakamoto commented:

> *A lot of people automatically dismiss e-currency as a lost cause because of all the companies that failed since the 1990s. I hope it's obvious it was only the centrally controlled nature of those systems that doomed them.*

This refers to the problem that someone has to issue the money. Until Bitcoin, this always required a central authority, like a central bank or corporation. In order to shut down a private currency, all that a government had to do was find the office where the currency was issued and shut it down. This is where proof-of-work comes in.

Proof-of-Work

Proof-of-work refers to a computing process that uses a defined amount of energy. This is a method whereby you can be absolutely certain that a computer did a certain amount of processing, effectively "proving" without a shadow of a doubt that you did a defined amount of work.

If you think about it, this has a lot of value. If you've spent much time on the internet (or being alive, for that matter), you've probably had to deal with people being fake. It's especially easy on the internet. But there's one thing on the internet you can't fake – mathematically provable energy consumption.

Bitcoin was inspired partly by Hashcash, a proof-of-work system designed by computer scientist Adam Back, one of the first people Satoshi Nakamoto contacted for help developing Bitcoin. Hashcash utilised proof-of-work as a defence against email spam attacks, in which thousands of emails flood an inbox. This protection was achieved by requiring any incoming email to contain a unique digital stamp that could only be generated by performing some operations with a computer processor. Such a stamp only takes a few seconds to generate, but it makes it much more difficult for a spammer to generate masses of emails.

The difficulty of proof-of-work can be adjusted almost infinitely to make the proofs harder and harder. As the Bitcoin network grows, the difficulty of the proof-of-work needed to acquire Bitcoin increases. There's a lot of complex mathematics behind all of this, and again, you don't need to understand it all. What is important to understand is that creating new Bitcoin requires work – very hard work, in fact: exactly the opposite of the old monetary system, where vast sums of money can simply be created out of nothing with a few strokes on a keyboard.

This work also secures the network against another problem that plagued previous attempts at digital currencies – the double spend. Double spending is the reason companies like Visa have to maintain anti-fraud departments with thousands of employees. A double spend occurs when someone makes a purchase and then reverses the transaction to spend the same funds twice. A classic example of a low-tech double-spending technique is using disappearing ink on cheques.

With proof-of-work, confirming a transaction requires so much work that it is almost impossible to reverse a transaction once it is confirmed – it would mean having to do the work all over again.

Blockchain

This security is further enhanced by the blockchain, which was an original invention by Satoshi Nakamoto. The blockchain makes it so that reversing a transaction would require not only repeating the work required to make a transaction but all of the work required to make every transaction since the transaction. Thus, Bitcoin transactions become more secure the older they are.

The blockchain is really nothing more than a glorified database – you could just as well call it an accounting book. The Bitcoin blockchain, for the most part, stores only one kind of data: transactions. Transactions are bundled into blocks, and the blocks are then "chained" together.

So what are the blocks made of, and how are they chained together?

The Bitcoin network gathers together a bundle of transactions: nothing more than pieces of information that say something along the lines of "Alice sent 10 Bitcoin to Bob." 10 Bitcoin are deducted from Alice's address and added to Bob's. Each transaction has an identification number, a timestamp, and some other data. All of these data are combined using a *hash*. A hash is an equation that condenses all of the data in the transaction into a unique string of numbers and letters 64 characters long. This is called a *hash ID*.

So a series of, say, 100 transactions might be grouped together. Indeed, if you were to write out all of this information in rows and columns, it would probably look rather like a block. Then another hash is used to combine all of the hash ID's of all the transactions to form another string, which is called a *block header*.

In addition to the transaction hash IDs, the block header must include the block header of the previous block. This is how the blocks are chained together. If any tiny detail of any transaction is modified, this will also change the block header. If any transaction in the history of all Bitcoin transactions is tampered with, the block header would no longer match, and the blockchain would be viewed as invalid by the network.

The block header must also include a number called a *nonce*. The nonce is a magic number that Bitcoin *miners* search for. The nonce is essential to how proof-of-work works; miners expend the effort to find it because if they do, they can collect the *block reward*, which is currently 6.25 Bitcoin.

Sometimes people say that Bitcoin miners are "solving" difficult mathematical problems. This isn't entirely true – they're just trying to guess a huge number.

This has a lot of complicated maths behind it, but it's enough to know that once a miner guesses the correct answer, it's very easy for everyone to verify that it's correct. It's a bit like searching for the right puzzle piece among millions of pieces – once someone finds it, there is no doubt that it's the right one because it fits.

At the same time, it's like they've found the key to a treasure box hidden inside the block, and the treasure box contains Bitcoin. Once the block is finished, the winning miner broadcasts it to the network. When they see the correct solution broadcast, they recognise that this unique block has been solved and the reward has been claimed. They also know that they will need the hash of the newly completed block to have a chance at solving the next block themselves.

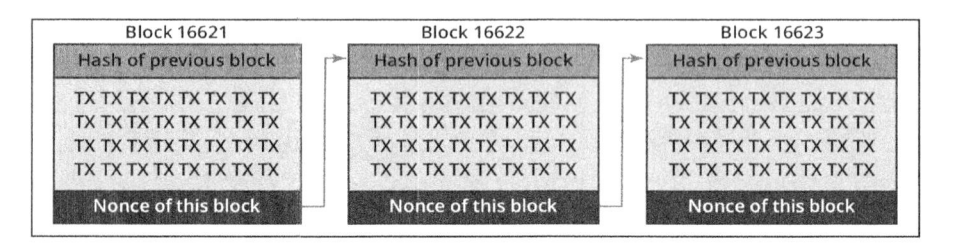

Block 16621	Block 16622	Block 16623
Hash of previous block	Hash of previous block	Hash of previous block
TX TX TX TX TX TX TX TX TX TX TX TX TX TX TX TX TX TX TX TX TX TX TX TX TX TX TX TX TX TX TX TX	TX TX TX TX TX TX TX TX TX TX TX TX TX TX TX TX TX TX TX TX TX TX TX TX TX TX TX TX TX TX TX TX	TX TX TX TX TX TX TX TX TX TX TX TX TX TX TX TX TX TX TX TX TX TX TX TX TX TX TX TX TX TX TX TX
Nonce of this block	Nonce of this block	Nonce of this block

Since it requires so much computation to find the nonce, the only way that a miner can "trick" the network is by creating two versions of the blockchain. To do this, the miner would have to control at least 51% of the network, so such an attack is called a *51% attack*.

To launch a 51% attack, you would have to control enough of the network to mine multiple consecutive blocks. At present, this would require many millions of dollars' worth of equipment and electricity, and even then, the risk can be avoided simply by waiting for a couple of hours before finalising a transaction. This is why many Bitcoin merchants require several blocks to be confirmed before finalising a transaction. This also illustrates the importance of decentralisation.

It's alright if you don't understand all this right away. It can take some time to sink in, and even many experts are still bewildered by it. What is important to realise is that it enables a group of people who don't trust each other to agree on who sent what to whom.

This solution in itself is revolutionising the financial industry. But combined with Bitcoin's political philosophy of decentralisation, it becomes a perfect storm of disruption for the entire world financial system. This decentralisation is embodied in the peer-to-peer nature of the network.

Peer-to-Peer Network

On November 6, 2008, Satoshi Nakamoto commented on the need for a peer-to-peer payment network:

> *Governments are good at cutting off the heads of centrally controlled networks like Napster, but pure P2P networks like Gnutella and Tor seem to be holding their own.*

Napster and Gnutella were both file-sharing protocols that allowed users to exchange any kind of data – including copyrighted films and music. This cut into the business of several large corporations, so Napster was shut down by court order. Soon after that, peer-to-peer networks like Gnutella became the platforms of choice for sharing files, where hundreds of people simultaneously shared small fractions of files. Since the users of the networks shared data directly with each other, there was no central server for governments to shut down.

These networks are difficult to shut down because responsibility for them is distributed between so many participants. To truly shut down the network, the government would have to track down every participant in the network and stop them from using it, which is more or less impossible logistically speaking.

With many peer-to-peer networks, this structure led to very bad quality because there was no central authority to prevent bad actors from abusing the network. This is exactly why proof-of-work was used in the case of Bitcoin. It places an economic cost on participation in the network, which makes attempts to abuse the network all but impossible. Abuse of the Bitcoin network was further discouraged by the addition of transaction fees, which both prevent spam (low-value transactions designed to clog the network) and provide additional incentives to Bitcoin miners, who secure the network.

One way to understand the strength of peer-to-peer networks is to compare trees and grass. If you cut a tree at a particular point, the whole tree will die. On the other hand, even when you cut grass into pieces, each one can continue to grow into a new network.

The most important point to understand here is that all of this technology allows the network to be *open*, which means that anyone can participate.

In the legacy banking system, if you happened to be in control of the bank's computer and your account contained £100,000, you could make yourself a millionaire just by adding a zero to your account balance.

This means you need to trust the bank because you obviously couldn't allow any Tom, Dick, or Harry to waltz in off the street and make whatever changes they wanted to the bank's database – there would be no way to ensure they were honest. With Bitcoin, ensuring the accuracy of balances and sending and receiving funds can be done without a trusted custodian. Anyone can mine, provided they have the equipment and electricity, and thus anyone has a chance at adding a block to the blockchain. Cryptography secures the integrity of the data, and proof-of-work and blockchain, combined with the peer-to-peer nature of the network, ensure that the data cannot be duplicated or reversed.

Peer-to-peer networks are sometimes explained with reference to the swarm effect, visible among some birds and fish. A large number of individual participants move in unison, operating according to simple rules and exhibits a sort of emergent consciousness.

The swarm seems to have a mind of its own, independent of the minds of individual participants. Each member of the swarm acts in its own interest, and yet somehow, the whole group moves as a harmonious whole, reminiscent of Adam Smith's *invisible hand* metaphor.

The story of Emily and Noah illustrates what can happen when a large group of people take the power of banks into their own hands. The banks never really had any power of their own beyond that which we gave them. The source of their power was the trust that so many people chose to put in them. If that power is returned to the people, it can do more than just protect our wealth – it can empower people to bring finance more into line with their values.

The borderless nature of cryptocurrency also means that a much larger swarm can form than ever before. The minimisation of trust enabled by cryptocurrency can allow large groups of people worldwide to collaborate in investing in a single project. We've already begun to see this with the rise of crowdfunding. Combined with social credit, this could signal the emergence of major advances in the ability to provide financing to people who deserve it and who may have been overlooked by the legacy financial system.

Unlocking Hidden Potential

Airbnb is a well-known example of how technology can be used to unlock latent wealth and achieve a higher degree of efficiency. In case you haven't heard of it, Airbnb is a room sharing platform that allows people to rent out rooms, houses, or even couches. The creators of this app understood that millions of people had empty rooms they'd like to rent out but were unable to find renters. In positioning themselves to connect people who need a place to stay with people who have a place to stay, Airbnb tapped into a vast gold mine.

Think of how many people in the world have an extra room they're willing to rent out or who go on holiday and want to rent out their flat while they're away. All of this latent space was wasted, so to speak, until a platform existed which allowed it to be marketed.

This is also the case with autonomous cars. Think of how much waste results from human-driven cars. When it comes to industrial management, it's well known that you want your machinery running as much as possible to achieve the maximum possible return on investment. And yet, most car owners only drive their cars for a few hours a day, at most. All of that time cars spend sitting in front of the house or office is lost efficiency.

Autonomous vehicles can drive for 24 hours a day. This can dramatically lower the cost of transportation and free up industrial resources for more important pursuits, like the development of renewable energy.

Cryptocurrency enables the deployment of this same logic on the level of finance. In the past, issuing securities was a very complex and expensive process that was only undertaken by large firms and with extensive regulatory oversight. Furthermore, most securities were only available to certain investors within single national markets.

In the past, all of this legal security was necessary to prevent fraud. Otherwise, any huckster or charlatan could sell us fake Apple shares or fraudulent investment certificates. And indeed, even with government oversight, scams like this have still seen some great losses.

But with secure, distributed cryptocurrency networks, we can issue secure certificates of ownership that can be effortlessly traded across the entire world market. This means money that once had to be tied up, sometimes for years, can be relatively liquid.

For example, consider a commercial property development. Let's say a construction company wants to finance a shopping mall. They can issue shares on a public blockchain like Bitcoin and then distribute rent profits to the owners of these certificates.

This enables the owners to freely sell their stake in the project whenever they want. In the past, an investor might have needed to tie up funds in such a project for several years. Now, investors of any size could theoretically buy and sell shares in a project at any time.

Because of the expense involved in issuing shares, only very large projects were securitised in this way in the past. Cryptocurrency lowers these costs dramatically, much in the same way that improvements in media technology have reduced the costs associated with media production and allowed YouTubers to compete with major media corporations. Now, ordinary people could directly share in financing a single residential property, like Emily and Noah's house.

The ability to cheaply and securely issue legal certificates of ownership also makes using collateral much easier. In the case of Noah and Emily, because they were trusted by their community, many of their friends and family were willing to back their aspirations to homeownership by putting up their own property as collateral. Before the rise of Bitcoin and blockchains, something like this would have been impossibly complex and expensive.

We've only just begun to explore the financial possibilities these new technologies have opened up.

It's currently very difficult to imagine what a society that isn't drowning in debt would look like. Sadly, the entire world is very much addicted to debt. But with the efficiency gains this technology enables, we may be able to unlock latent potential stores of wealth, much in the same way that Airbnb unlocked efficiency gains in the form of unused space. This could go a long way towards eliminating the addiction to debt and the financial crises that inevitably accompany the excessive build-up of debt.

There are a number of elements of cryptocurrency that make a story like Emily and Noah's possible. One is the fact that cryptocurrency enables peer-to-peer finance on a never before imagined scale. Another is that it can dramatically increase the liquidity of investments and enable better collateralisation through tokenisation. And finally, cryptocurrency opens up vast new stores of data for analytics because cryptography can allow financial records to be made publicly verifiable without compromising privacy or security. This data can be used for more effective credit analysis, which eliminates the need for the specialised investment analysis of bankers, meaning that non-experts can effectively invest directly in the individuals or businesses seeking a loan.

2. Amadou Touré

The High Cost of Poverty

Amadou felt a sense of dread when he saw the storm clouds on the horizon. He hoped and prayed that it was just an overcast day and the clouds would soon blow over. There was no point in talking about it – there was no turning back. Besides, the passengers could hardly hear each other over the drone of the boat's motor. They'd heard the stories, and they all knew how it might end when they stepped aboard. It was a risk they were willing to take.

Amadou was born in Guinea, West Africa. He started working at the age of 8 in illegal gold mines. The hours were long, the work was tiring, and the pay was low, but he was happy because he could help his mother pay for the household expenses.

When he was twelve years old, the Guinean government granted a concession to a foreign company to mine the area of the river where he worked. Government soldiers arrived one day and began tearing apart the camp where he and his mother lived, stealing whatever they found of value and arresting anyone who protested. Amadou and his mother fled to the capital, Conakry.

Amadou soon found work as a courier in the city's market, running handcarts full of plantains, foam mattresses and other goods between the stalls. At first, he rented a cart by the day but soon started saving up to buy his own. After six months of hard work and economising, he'd finally saved enough to buy the cart when Guinea suffered a bout of hyperinflation. The value of his savings was wiped out. On the bright side, he found work pushing carts loaded up with bricks of millions of Guinean francs, now nearly worthless.

He began again, but this time was careful to keep his savings in Senegalese currency, the CFA franc, which tended to be more stable. After a year, he bought his own cart. His earnings increased, and at the age of sixteen, he opened a shop of his own. It was a simple life, but he was happy and even got married.

Not long after Amadou's wedding, the country's president was ousted in a coup, and the situation went from bad to worse. Police salaries, which were low before the unrest, were now not paid at all. Before the coup, the police would come once a month demanding bribes – after the coup, they came every week. The bribes consumed the small profits that Amadou earned from his shop, forcing him to sell it to cover his expenses.

Feeding his family from what he'd received from selling his business, he watched his financial reserves dwindling every day. All his neighbours were struggling except for those receiving support from relatives in America or Europe. Soon, it was only through the generosity of these fortunate families that Amadou and his family were able to survive. He had no choice; he borrowed from everyone willing to lend him the money he needed to pay for the journey to Europe.

Amadou spent the first leg of the trip choking on dust in the back of six different trucks crossing the Sahara. He ate only one meal of dry bread and canned sardines per day. After three weeks of arduous travel, he arrived in Tunisia, tired but no less determined to reach his goal.

In Tunis, the country's capital city, he met several other Guineans who helped him find a smuggler organising a clandestine voyage to Italy. He spent nearly two months sleeping in an abandoned warehouse, waiting for the boat to embark. When he saw the boat, he immediately had a bad feeling. Something told him not to get on, to run in the other direction. It was a small fishing boat, sitting low in the water under the weight of at least two hundred men, women, and children. He heard the sound of several infants wailing somewhere amid the seething mass.

He suppressed his sense of foreboding and stepped aboard. He'd come too far to turn back now.

He didn't know why he felt so bad about it. It was a sunny day with a light breeze. It should take just 36 hours to reach Italy.

After some 12 hours at sea, everyone had grown accustomed to the waves crashing over the side. As the boat began to fill with water, Amadou and several others used empty water bottles in what felt like the futile task of bailing out the boat by hand. No matter how much water they threw overboard, the level stayed the same. Amadou shivered – the biting cold was unlike anything he'd experienced in Guinea. His feet were soaking wet and swollen.

As the sun went down, ominous dark clouds appeared, and the waves grew higher. The wailing of the infants rose, and some passengers began to vomit, filling the boat with a nauseating smell. Lightning flashed. The water was up to their knees and rising despite their bailing. Suddenly, the motor stopped, and a sense of peace descended, just as suddenly broken by the howling wind, the driving rain and a crash of thunder that filled them all with fear.

Shouting at each other, the smugglers struggled to restart the motor. As they drifted, the swells rose higher, and the boat rocked more violently. Helpless, Amadou watched a massive wave hit the side of the boat and felt the world turn upside down.

He could see nothing but darkness as he went under, and the saltwater stung his eyes. He felt flailing limbs hitting him from all directions as he fought to get back to the surface.

Having grown up next to the river as a gold miner, he was a strong swimmer. Surfacing, he heard screams all around. He saw the boat floating upside down and clutched at a length of the boat's rail.

Amadou saw a woman nearby gasping for breath and struggling to keep herself and her baby above the water. He swam across to help them reach the capsized boat, but the mother was in a state of panic. She clutched at him frantically, dragging him under. Already out of breath, he gasped involuntarily, filling his lungs with water. Coughing and choking, he swam back to the boat to catch his breath. He looked for the woman again, but she and her baby had disappeared.

The screams continued around him, but he was barely able to keep his own head above water. If he could rest for a moment and catch his breath, he told himself, he could come back and try to help. He scrambled up onto the underside of the boat but quickly found he needed all of his energy just to cling to the keel as it rose and fell on the waves.

Soon the screams and cries stopped, and the storm subsided. When dawn appeared, Amadou found himself one of about twenty survivors clinging to the boat – all that remained of the more than two hundred passengers. Amadou shivered, his frigid hands unable even to clutch the boat. The sun rose, and he had never been more grateful for its warmth, but now they became acutely aware that they had no water.

Amadou's lips were parched and cracked from the salty water he'd swallowed the night before. He soon felt so tired from dehydration that he could hardly move. The first day passed with the survivors in deep shock. The next day, they resolved to do something, but all attempts to flip the boat over failed.

While diving in search of the radio, which they never found, they discovered a fuel canister connected to the boat and still containing fuel. They spent the rest of the day searching in vain for a match or a lighter to make a signal fire.

On the fifth day at sea, they managed to ignite a fuel-soaked rag with a spark produced by striking the propeller with a piece of the boat's rail.

They tore up one of the few life jackets and threw the bits into the flames. Acrid, black smoke rose to the sky, visible for miles around. After several hours, when the fuel was used up, the fire was out, and they were close to losing hope, a ship appeared.

It was the Spanish coast guard. The refugees had drifted hundreds of miles toward Majorca. As the crew of the rescue ship helped them aboard, Amadou was despondent. He thought he would be overjoyed to have a sip of water, but felt almost totally indifferent as to whether he lived or died. His thoughts kept returning to the passengers who hadn't made it. *Why them*, he thought, *and not me?*

It was several weeks before he regained his bearings. He spent most of his days expressionlessly watching the activity around him. When offered food by the immigrant detention camp's staff, he ate slowly and without emotion. But soon, he remembered his family at home and the money he had borrowed to make it this far. Slowly, Amadou's resolve returned, and he started to move.

The first weeks were lost in bureaucracy, but as soon as he received his refugee documents, he went out onto the streets to search for work. He quickly found the Guinean community, who helped him find a job harvesting tomatoes. The pay was five cents per kilo and worked out at about 15 euros for a day's work. At the end of the month, he was able to send 200 euros home to his family.

After the transfer fee, there were 185 euros left, 100 of which went to cover his debts for the journey. After two months, the tomato harvest ended, and winter began, leaving him with no work. He had picked up a little French while growing up in Guinea, so he took his earnings and purchased a bus ticket to Geneva, where he'd heard that some relatives from his tribe had found work.

In Geneva, he tracked down his distant cousin, Oumar, who'd been in the city for longer than anyone. Oumar lent Amadou the money to get a driver's licence so that he could drive a taxi. He also provided him with a car, for which Amadou paid his cousin a proportion of his earnings. Amadou was thrilled – after he paid Oumar, he would be getting 30 euros a day, double what he'd earned picking tomatoes.

Getting the licence, however, was a dizzying maze of bureaucracy. Amadou used the opportunity to improve his limited reading skills and his French. He only had a few years of schooling, but he'd learned to read to do the bookkeeping while running his shop. After struggling for months with the Swiss highway code and taking late-night driving lessons with Oumar, he emerged triumphant from his driving test.

He was working nights, sometimes driving 12 hours a day, for which he was making 30 to 40 Swiss francs after Oumar took his share. He couldn't send all of this to his family as he had other debts to Oumar. He was happy to send them 150 francs every two weeks, but he started to feel very lonely. With the money he sent, his family bought a phone and internet credit, and Amadou saw his son walking for the first time during a video call. He made friends in Geneva but hardly had time to do anything but work. He desperately wanted to go home and see his family, but he had no idea how he could earn a living if he did.

Even if he saved up and opened another business, most of his profits would end up lining the pockets of corrupt officials. So he quietly carried on.

Sometimes he would chat with his passengers to ease the loneliness. He often drove in the same neighbourhoods and occasionally gave rides to the same people. One of his regular customers was an elderly Dutch gentleman who he sometimes drove to various UN offices around the city. His name was Lars, and he and Amadou got on quite well.

Lars was on an assignment with an NGO that was collaborating with the UN. Like Amadou, he missed his family. He'd been working in

Geneva for quite some time and could only go home once a month. Amadou sympathised with him, explaining that he hadn't seen his family in almost two years.

When Amadou chatted with his other customers, very few of them knew anything about Africa. By contrast, Lars was unusually interested in Africa; he asked pointed questions and even seemed to know all the different cities and tribes in Guinea. On one of their trips, he asked what tribe Amadou belonged to. Amadou replied that he belonged to the Loma people.

"You mean you speak the Loma language?" Lars asked.

"Yes, that's my mother language," he said, "but I grew up mostly speaking Kissi and Susu with my friends. I know some Fulani and Malinké too." Lars was amazed.

"You know, we could really use someone with your language skills. I'm working on a project that's meant to be deployed in West Africa, and we've been struggling to find someone who can help us work with the Loma population."

"Well, I'd like to help, but I am the only one supporting my family right now."

Lars paused for a moment, then said, "I'll talk to the director and see what he thinks." Amadou expressed his appreciation, dropped Lars off at the destination, and thought no more of it.

Two days later, Lars rang. He sounded excited. He wanted Amadou to come to his office and meet his team.

At the office, Lars introduced Amadou to everyone and told him more about their project. They were working on a digital identity system and planned to deploy a pilot program in Liberia. They explained that everyone would be assigned a unique ID number in a database that they could use for all government services, including voting and receiving aid from international agencies.

Amadou remembered aid organisations handing out medicine and how some of the families in his area would get more than their share by sending all of the children separately, each claiming to be from a different family, and then sell the medicine. He also remembered that other families were unable to get assistance as a result. If this new system could stop that, it would be a good thing, he thought.

Lars explained that they were having difficulty trying to coordinate with some Loma tribal leaders. They didn't trust outsiders.

Amadou tried to explain, "You see, the Loma have had some terrible experiences since the time of the civil war. They probably think that you are trying to collect information on them to give to the government."

"It's actually just the opposite. We recognise the abuses of the government, and we're trying to make sure everyone, including the Loma, gets their rights," Lars replied.

Amadou was stunned when they offered him a job as an interpreter. The salary was low by Swiss standards – it was paid through the branch office in Liberia and worked out to around 600 dollars a month. But for Amadou, it felt like winning the lottery. And he'd be able to see his family.

With his debt to Oumar fully paid off, he travelled to Liberia with Lars and his team and got straight to work. As it turned out, he helped to translate Mandé as well as Loma, Susu and Kissi because Mandé was quite similar to the Malinké he knew. In village after village, he met with elders and explained the plans to them – how this new system would ensure their votes were counted, how it could prove their ownership over land and prevent anyone from forcing them off of their land, and ensure that aid destined for them would not be embezzled by the government.

With Amadou's help, the program progressed quickly in the remote hinterlands of Liberia. And although he was very busy with his work in Liberia, he had time to travel to Conakry once a month and see his family.

As he came to understand the technology his colleagues were working on, he started to ask questions about its origin. Lars explained that it had begun as a system for the transfer of money and told him the story of Bitcoin. When Amadou heard that you could use Bitcoin to send money anywhere in the world, his first question was about the fees. He realised it was much cheaper than the methods he and the Guinean community in Geneva had been using, and he immediately saw an opportunity. So many families in Conakry received money abroad, and here was a chance to transfer the money for less than a tenth of what they'd been paying.

He contacted Oumar in Geneva, got in touch with the Guinean community, and then spoke with his brother-in-law, Babacar, in Conakry. He sent him a small amount of money to get started, and they began offering low-priced exchange services. Other families followed suit. The savings amounted to around 100,000 Guinean francs a month for most families – about 10 euros – but for many in Guinea, that was equivalent to a week's wages.

As the Bitcoin business in Conakry continued to grow, Amadou had another idea. He remembered Babacar was a renowned drummer – he'd played at their wedding. Like most Guineans, he was having trouble finding work, and the income from their money transfer business was quite modest. So Amadou suggested he start an online, West African drumming school.

Babacar enlisted the help of an internet-savvy relative, and they set about building a website and advertising his classes on Facebook.

Since he could receive payments from all over the world without any trouble, he soon had five students – one from Japan, one from Sweden, two from France and one from Romania. His English was limited, but the rhythms spoke for themselves. The classes were quite cheap, and it would have been unthinkable for him to integrate a payment platform to process such small payments with Guinea's ramshackle banking system, but with cryptocurrency, it was very easy.

With a few good reviews on their Facebook page, more students soon followed; some were even interested in travelling to Guinea and learning in person. One of the best things about his business was that not having a bank account meant the corrupt police were unaware that he had a business at all – otherwise, he would surely have been suffocated by bribes, like most of Guinea's other small business owners.

As the pilot project progressed in Liberia, Amadou continually shared the results with his friends and relatives in Guinea via WhatsApp. Since many tribes overlapped the Guinea-Liberia border, word spread quickly among relatives. Amadou longed to implement some of the changes he'd seen in Liberia in Guinea, but the government was very hostile to any such reforms.

Then, one day, explosions and gunshots were heard around the presidential palace in Conakry. Soon, an army general appeared on television and announced that the military had seized power in a coup.

This was not a particularly unusual occurrence in Guinea; this time, however, it was different. Masses of people appeared in the streets demanding elections. The general ordered his troops to fire on the crowd, but seeing the people were unarmed, the soldiers refused. The protestors then stormed the main police station, the presidential palace, and the television station.

Leaders of the protest formed a joint council with the military and struggled to form a government. In an attempt to mediate the situation and prevent the talks from descending into violence, the UN envoy to Guinea called Lars and requested his help organising the election. Past elections had seen extensive fraud, and neither side trusted the other to appoint officials to tally the votes.

Lars, Amadou, and their team travelled from Liberia to Guinea. The interest groups involved in the talks were mainly from the Malinké, Baga, and Fulani tribes, so as a Susu, Amadou was seen as neutral. He explained to the different parties how the system worked and how the votes were instantly stored on a secure network maintained in dozens of countries – with no possibility for anyone to tamper with the results. He also explained that each vote was connected to the voter's fingerprint, so it would be impossible to fake.

All the parties agreed, and the huge task of assigning digital identities to all 10 million of the country's adult population began. It was more than triple what they had accomplished in Liberia, but their experience had prepared them well. Amadou was tasked with training a group of volunteers from each prefecture, who were then dispatched to establish registration stations in the communes.

Occasionally, he had to travel to remote areas to help smooth out conflicts and explain the benefits of the system. Once people understood the reasoning behind the technology, it wasn't hard to convince them to register. After eight months of frantic and exhausting work, they were ready for the election.

Although everything went smoothly, forming a government was still a chaotic process: however, the new digital identity system lifted a great administrative load from the resource-strapped country.

Once the registrations were complete, other uses for the digital identities began to appear. Guinea had very little in the way of a banking system, so mobile payments were very popular, and telecom companies integrated the digital identities into mobile payment systems. With the growing popularity of mobile payments, ordinary Guineans suddenly had credit histories. Before, banks had requested documentation from those seeking loans – proof of income, utility bills, deeds of title, etc. – and almost no one had any.

But the new identity system gave Guineans the option to give the banks access to their data. Thus, lenders could find creditworthy individuals much more easily using data analysis, and new projects started to spring up at an unprecedented rate.

The leaders of the protest movements also demanded that licences and permits and all payments to the government be recorded on the public record. Corrupt officials demanding bribes were met with mobs of angry citizens who demonstrated that they had already paid their fees by referring to the public record. With the upsurge of investment in the country, government revenues increased, the salaries of police and government officials went up, and the demands for bribes became increasingly rare.

Amadou could not believe his good fortune – not only had he been able to return home to help raise his son, but he had also participated in the transformation he saw sweeping through his country. With the improving economy and reduced corruption, more and more Guineans started returning home to their families and using the savings and skills acquired abroad to start their own businesses.

He sometimes wondered if it was destiny that he survived on the boat all those years ago. In any case, it seemed that his children would never have to go through what he went through, and for that, Amadou was deeply grateful.

✴ ✴ ✴

Trustless Government

In the story of Emily and Noah, we saw how Bitcoin could disrupt traditional banking institutions, removing them as middlemen. Amadou's story illustrates how something similar can happen with government institutions. So how did Bitcoin enable this?

At first, Bitcoin was intended purely to solve the problem of trusted third parties in digital payments. It solved that problem very well, but as people began to study Bitcoin more closely, they realised transactional data was not the only data a blockchain could store – it could store *any* kind of data. Bitcoin includes a function called OP_RETURN, which can be used to embed additional data in transactions.

Satoshi actually even included a message with the first block ever created – the genesis block:

> *The Times, 03/Jan/2009, Chancellor on brink of second bailout for banks.*

This was a headline from the financial crisis announcing the creation of more money to bail out the banks. This leaves little doubt about Satoshi's motivation, but it also illustrates that Bitcoin can carry other types of data. Since it can store data on an open network in a way that cannot be faked – it's ideally suited to be used for anything that people might try to fake.

One of the first experiments was with property deeds of ownership. Data representing all the relevant details – property ID number, buyer, seller, location of the property, etc. – could be saved on the Bitcoin blockchain and thus immutably preserved.

People soon realised that this could work just as well with licences, university diplomas, notarised documents, ballots, and just about any other document. This could save a huge amount of work and paper by enabling the secure digitisation of documents. Buying a house, or even a car, can be a very complex process, usually involving the government.

The government's role is necessary to confirm that the seller of the car really owns it and to transfer the ownership of the car to the new buyer. In this way, if the car is stolen, it is possible to prove who the rightful owner is. Just as Bitcoin eliminated the need for a bank to guard the authenticity of account balances, other blockchain applications could reduce or eliminate the need for trusted institutions to guarantee the authenticity of documents.

Fighting Corruption

The great hope is that digitising these administrative functions could both enable and force governments to be more transparent and efficient. Low-income countries are severely limited in terms of governance – they simply can't afford to pay the salaries of enough officials to maintain functional bureaucracies. Those officials that do receive salaries are paid so little that they often turn to bribes just to make a decent living.

Corruption is one of the major factors that drives immigrants to risk their lives trying to reach Europe. It's extremely difficult for entrepreneurs to succeed when already tight budgets are burdened by bribery and corruption. In many countries, the only people able to effectively run businesses are those connected with the ruling elite.

Even anti-corruption drives cost money that many countries just don't have. Since corruption hampers economic growth, it becomes a vicious cycle. Digitising and automating permits, licences, and government documents could go a long way towards breaking this cycle. An immutable record of all payments would remove the pretext for soliciting bribes. The workload associated with recording, authenticating, and filling out documents would also decrease.

This presents a much bigger challenge to wealthy countries, where automation threatens millions of jobs in the coming years. Finding work for all those affected will be a colossal challenge. In low-income countries, however, it means governments that are already stretched thin may be better able to focus their limited resources. It could make it possible to pay civil servants better salaries and reduce the pressure to take bribes.

This goes not only for government services but also for many legal services, like escrow. Escrow is an essential function of property markets, but it can involve large sums of money and, as such, requires extensive security guarantees. In the United States, for example, the title and escrow industry is worth over 25 billion dollars every year. This industry requires extensive training and legal infrastructure, much of which can now be replaced with free, open-source software.

These savings can be realised in politics as well as business. An election conducted with secure digital identities based on distributed ledgers like the Bitcoin blockchain could be much more affordable and much more resistant to fraud. It is theoretically possible to embed secure identifying information on a distributed ledger, such as fingerprints and retinal scans. The development of such systems is already underway.

Blockchain vs Bitcoin

Bitcoin has always been a technology intent on challenging the mainstream. It's understandable, then, that the mainstream would be sceptical of Bitcoin and other cryptocurrencies. And one of the clearest manifestations of this scepticism is the focus on blockchain rather than Bitcoin.

This emphasis on the blockchain, which is only one component of Bitcoin, as outlined in Chapter 1, is an attempt to try to remove everything that certain people dislike about Bitcoin while keeping the parts they like. This is not entirely possible, however. People who benefit from the current system don't want to see it change because they'll lose their privilege in the process. Bitcoin removes a great deal of power from the hands of the current elite in both finance and government. The decentralisation and distribution of authority are essential to Bitcoin's value proposition. A blockchain, without openness and decentralisation, is little more than a very expensive database.

With issues like corruption or electoral fraud, networks must be open and decentralised, meaning that no centralised authority may have power over them. Electoral fraud is most often carried out by incumbent governments, so you certainly don't want the government to be in control of the system.

For this reason, the importance of confidence in the integrity of a blockchain-based network is paramount, especially with sensitive political data like votes. Proof-of-work systems like Bitcoin use economic incentives to provide security, and as of 2020, Bitcoin is the most secure decentralised blockchain network in existence due to its sheer size. The amount of miners maintaining the Bitcoin blockchain means that any attempts to tamper with the data would be prohibitively expensive. The Ethereum network is a close runner-up and has been used for United Nations trials related to governance initiatives like those described in Amadou's story.

Some important differences between Bitcoin and Ethereum highlight an ideological fault line in the world of cryptocurrency.

While Ethereum is currently based on a proof-of-work algorithm, there are plans to switch over to another system of security guarantees called proof-of-stake.

This has raised concerns because such models have been criticised on several theoretical grounds. This topic will be examined at greater length in Chapter 3. For now, when we imagine that distributed networks may form the foundation of future governmental systems, design choices take on tremendous importance.

The advantage of open-source software here is clear. Russia also had plans to store electoral data on a blockchain, but an independent security auditor found that the public-private key pairs were too small to provide adequate security. As such, votes could be hacked using a standard personal computer. It's unclear whether this design flaw was intentional, but there are certainly plenty of individuals in the world who have no interest in seeing more transparent, tamper-proof data structures.

With time, as this technology becomes more widespread, it will become increasingly clear that governments who oppose independent standards of transparency have something to hide. This could undermine the legitimacy of corrupt governments and empower the oppressed around the world.

Putting Billions in the Pockets of the World's Poor

Remittances worldwide have become an essential source of income for millions of people. The fees sent home by immigrant workers average around 5 to 15 per cent of the total amount of money sent. This doesn't seem like much, but considering the massive volume of global remittance flows, it all adds up. According to the United Nations, it amounted to more than £19 billion in 2018 alone.

The people receiving these funds are often among the most impoverished on earth. Now, with the existence of cryptocurrency, there is no excuse for this. Money can be sent and received for virtually nothing now. That means that with the adoption of cryptocurrencies, £19 billion can be put directly in the pockets of the world's poorest, almost overnight. This could mean huge improvements in quality of life.

Furthermore, consider the cumulative time savings – many of the world's unbanked have to travel a considerable distance to reach the nearest bank or money transfer agent. In the West, we take for granted having all of these facilities on our doorsteps, but for many people in the world, going to a bank can mean a journey of several hours or more. It can also mean paying for transport both ways. Although the cost of transport might be no more than a few pounds, this can be a considerable sum for those with low incomes.

With cryptocurrency, it's possible to transfer money directly from one mobile phone to another across international borders. Mobile internet is already available even in many remote areas of Africa, and plans are underway to extend this access even further. The rise of cryptocurrency means money can be transferred as easily and as cheaply as any other type of information.

Technological Leapfrogging

In the past, building bank infrastructure was quite an expensive proposition. You had to install dedicated connections, train specialised personnel, and open physical branches. The sheer lack of capital in places like Africa made this unprofitable, and so millions were unable to access financial services, resulting in a vicious cycle of poverty.

With the rise of affordable mobile internet and cryptocurrency, millions in Africa will suddenly have access to the same level of services available in highly industrialised countries. The lack of infrastructure can actually become an advantage, as it leads to faster rates of adoption of new technology. This phenomenon is sometimes called technological leapfrogging.

In wealthy countries, consumers already have access to less efficient legacy systems, and therefore have little incentive to trouble themselves learning new technologies. In many parts of Africa, however, these new, more efficient technologies are the only option available, and so people adopt new and superior technologies at a much faster rate, leading to efficiency gains.

This was very well exemplified by the case of M-Pesa in Kenya. Surprisingly, Kenya has one of the highest rates of mobile payment adoption in the world. This is largely because bank transfer systems were relatively undeveloped, so there was a clear need to develop mobile payment systems. Initially, it started when people began using prepaid mobile credits as a form of cash, but telecom providers quickly caught on and offered direct cash transfers between subscribers. Today, almost 50% of Kenya's GDP is processed by mobile payments, the highest rate in the world.

We may see a similar scenario with cryptocurrency in places like Africa. Zimbabwe recently suffered from a severe case of hyperinflation, and in the aftermath, Bitcoin has grown dramatically in popularity. Consumers in countries with relatively stable currencies don't have the same motivation to learn how to work with cryptocurrency as those in a country where the currency collapses.

As cryptocurrency adoption continues to grow, so will the value of the overall market. This can also be a mechanism for levelling the playing field of the global economy. Adopting commerce in cryptocurrency can greatly facilitate cross-border commerce. The global economy has been growing steadily more service-based. Easy cross-border payments literally open up a world of possibilities for commerce.

3. Adriana Pereira

Fighting Crime on New Frontiers

Adriana came from a working-class family and grew up in one of Rio de Janeiro's *favelas*. From an early age, she was fascinated by courtroom dramas on TV, and since crime and violence were rampant in her neighbourhood, she developed a sort of admiration for the work of the police and courts. She was an unusually gifted student, and after secondary school earned a scholarship to study law and criminal justice at the University of Sao Paulo, where she graduated with honours.

After graduation, Adriana was offered a job by Brazil's Council for Financial Activities Control (FAC). She started out as a legal attaché analysing and tracing counterfeit banknotes. Her job training included specialised forensics courses where she learned to identify the materials used when counterfeiting money. She had a natural aptitude for it and was soon called in to assist law enforcement with their investigations. She worked closely with investigators, using the results of forensic analysis to justify surveillance of the buyers as a means of catching the counterfeiters.

As soon as one operation was over, another would spring up. Anti-counterfeiting technologies were developing fast, and twice within five years, the government introduced new banknotes based on recommendations from Adriana's department. All the same, new counterfeiters appeared with more sophisticated methods. The fakes became almost indistinguishable from authentic banknotes, causing billions in financial damages. It was an exhausting and seemingly never-ending arms race.

When Adriana first learned about Bitcoin and blockchain technology, she was intrigued. And, as soon as she understood how it worked, she realised that a cryptographically secured currency would be impossible to fake. At last, she saw a clear solution to the problems she struggled with every day and began to discuss the possibilities of a digital currency with her colleagues.

Some police are keen to keep their jobs at any cost, but Adriana fought to make hers obsolete. She didn't enjoy it that much, anyway. Yes, it was rewarding to lock up criminals, many of whom were involved in other crimes, but she could never quite shake the feeling that what the counterfeiters were doing wasn't so different from what the banks were doing. And yet, they weren't allowed to arrest or prosecute the bankers.

As cryptocurrency grew in popularity, she pressured her boss, Silvio, the head of the FAC, to write to Brazil's National Congress. She was called to testify and made a compelling case for adopting cryptocurrency technology. Based on her testimony, along with those of other experts, the government signed into law a set of regulations legalising cryptocurrencies and establishing a state-managed cryptocurrency. Brazil made history as one of the first countries to go fully digital.

This proved to be a huge boon for commerce as it not only enabled budding micro-entrepreneurs to reach larger markets but also had major benefits for the police. The vast majority of crimes had been committed using cash, which was untraceable, but with digital currency, there was always a paper trail. Street muggings dropped dramatically as thefts became much more traceable. And as Adriana had expected, the problem of counterfeiting was completely eliminated.

As counterfeiting declined, the number of cryptocurrency-related fraud cases increased, and Silvio approached her to head the FAC's new cryptocurrency division. She was fascinated by the technology, so it was a natural fit. And so, she set out to tame the wild world of cryptocurrencies.

Here she faced new challenges – criminals were using cryptocurrency to operate in new ways, and crime seemed to be migrating online. One of the most common problems was scammers making outlandish promises to unsuspecting investors to steal their funds. Some of these cases were outright Ponzi schemes, while others were just poorly planned and executed business ventures. One of the biggest challenges Adriana faced was the international nature of many of the scams. It was next to impossible to bring the scammers to justice unless they were located in Brazil. Since money could now flow so easily across national borders, Adriana realised a much greater degree of international cooperation was necessary.

The FAC's exhausting process of establishing partnerships with police forces around the world began. Adriana participated in making recommendations for an international treaty that was signed by 189 of the United Nations member states and made prosecuting and extraditing cryptocurrency criminals much easier. But a pattern gradually emerged – as much progress as they made against cryptocurrency-related crime, the criminals still managed to find safe havens. Rogue states with tight budgets and corrupt governments were happy to host the criminals in exchange for a share of the loot.

They realised there was only so much law enforcement could do to stop the criminals, so the focus shifted from law enforcement to education. Adriana represented Brazil at the Nairobi Summit on Cryptocurrency Crime and Fraud.

In partnership with the private sector, the delegates agreed to establish an accredited advisory board with a vetting process for cryptocurrency-related business ventures. Projects wishing to achieve credibility would have to undergo this process, and the authenticity of their certification could be proven with a cryptographically secured signature that would accompany all of their communications and promotional materials.

Many of the claims made by fraudsters were not difficult to disprove, but investors could easily get caught up in flashy marketing campaigns promising massive wealth. With the new international certification scheme, investors could simply check whether a project or digital asset had been verified by the International Cryptocurrency Fraud Prevention Committee (ICFPC).

Another pressing concern in the cryptocurrency crime division was money laundering. Weapons smugglers, human traffickers, hackers, and militant groups were all able to expand their online operations as the circulation of cryptocurrency increased. Again, since this was an international problem, it required an international solution.

As Adriana travelled around the world meeting prosecutors and law enforcement, it became clear that they had to develop a common resource for tracking funds involved in money laundering operations.

They met with consultants from leading technology firms, and a plan was hatched to develop a dynamic database for tracking financial flows. Law enforcement from around the world could mark funds that were known to be connected to crimes. Agreements were signed with major exchanges and miners to integrate their trading data into the database so that when these funds were traded for another currency, that currency would be marked as well.

In this way, funds connected to criminal activity could be traced more effectively, and even if they couldn't be found, it was possible to find those who purchased the currency from them. This at least gave police a starting point for investigations.

When the new system was finished, they had an advanced interface with visualisations of cryptocurrency flows all over the world. AI-driven algorithms signalled when they detected suspicious behaviour, and alerts popped up any time funds associated with a particular crime moved.

The entire database was searchable and programmable, so it could be customised for individual cases. With this marvel of international coordination, cryptocurrency-related crime dropped sharply, but once again, the criminals adapted. They began to favour anonymous cryptocurrencies more and more. It was still possible to track movements in and out of the currencies, but this required more old-fashioned detective work, understanding where income came from and noting any unusual purchases or unexplained wealth.

It was relatively easy to restrict the use of anonymous currencies from legitimate businesses, and so the operational capacity of criminals declined considerably. This led to the growth of a sort of parallel economy used by illegal actors.

This is the problem Adriana was struggling with when, one day, she was called into an investigation as a consultant. A prostitute had been hospitalised after a severe beating by her pimp, and she wanted to file a report against him. When the police began to question her about her pimp, she described what sounded like the use of an anonymous cryptocurrency.

The girl was originally from Colombia, but when she was 14, a man had approached her, offering her work in Brazil in a restaurant. The salary he promised was better than anything in her town in Colombia. Since her family was impoverished, she accepted. But as soon as she crossed the border, the man took her passport and forced her to work as a prostitute. He denied her access to a phone, wouldn't let her call her family and threatened to kill her if she tried to run away.

The beating had occurred when he caught her with a phone. He'd taken her to the hospital because he was afraid that without treatment, she might not be able to work anymore. The staff had sensed something was wrong and called hospital security for assistance. The girl was eager to have him locked up, but she was also petrified of what he might do if he knew she was helping the police.

She explained that her pimp was just one member of a larger organisation. The different members had different roles – some were lookouts, some solicited customers, some provided security, some handled logistics with cash, weapons, or girls. The organised crime unit was already on the scene taking her statement when Adriana arrived. This gang had been known to the unit for some time, but recently they'd become more sophisticated, better organised, and well-armed. Adriana wanted to find out if cryptocurrency was somehow enabling the growth of the gang and what could be done to stop it. Adriana asked the girl whether the pimp had dealings with digital currencies.

The first step was to find the girl's pimp. Based on her statement, the police raided a building where he had been working. There were several more girls there and a cache of weapons, but the girls were too afraid to talk to the police, who were forced to release them. They did, however, find a laptop and several phones with cryptocurrency wallets.

Adriana cross-referenced the transactions against the international database and found that the funds had been transferred to a series of wallets before finally appearing in a Hong Kong exchange. She called the Hong Kong cryptocurrency bureau and requested records on the exchange.

Adriana asked them for a list of the addresses used to buy the anonymous currency with *e-reals*, Brazil's digital currency. She noted the amounts of the purchases and then went to the pimp, who was still in the local jail.

"Where did you send all your profits from the girls?" she asked.

"To the boss," he replied.

"Who's the boss?" she asked.

"Nobody knows who the boss is."

"How did you start working for him, then?"

"Someone approached me and told me he could get me set up working; help me to get merchandise, weapons, and girls. He connected me with the boss. The boss connected me with a guy in procurement. Me, I just handle the customers."

"Procurement?"

"Yeah, he sources the girls."

"Why don't you just keep the money for yourself?"

"If anyone steps out of line, the boss takes them out. Sometimes he offers bonuses to get rid of guys who don't pay their dues or who decide to go it alone. That's why I stick with the boss."

She asked him more about the way he did business. He was eager to get out, so he cooperated gladly on the promise of a shorter sentence. But all of his communications with the boss were encrypted, and all of the money sent to and from the boss was from anonymous addresses.

The pimp had been advertising his girls online. The boss used the online portal to monitor all the girls, to make sure that no one cheated him. The customers would make a cryptocurrency deposit to an account, and only then would they gain access to the girls. Adriana decided to check some of the ads.

On a whim, she used a style analysis tool to check the description written in the advert. To her surprise, she found similar adverts not only in Rio but in cities across Europe, Asia, and South America.

She called some of the police departments in the cities with matching ads, and they all told similar stories. They would catch human traffickers, but none of them had any money on them. And as soon as they were arrested, new, well-funded traffickers quickly appeared to take their place.

Adriana understood that these local arrests were just minions. To stop them, they had to cut off the head of the operation.

She accessed the cryptocurrency database again and narrowed the search filter to the cities where she'd found matching adverts.

A clear pattern emerged: in every city where the ads were active, there were also payments going back to a series of addresses.

Many of the addresses were connected to a known address belonging to a cryptocurrency exchange in Hong Kong.

She contacted the Hong Kong cryptocurrency crime bureau, requested information from the exchange and gave them a series of transaction IDs. They called back the next day and told her that the transactions had been deposited in the account of a well-known antiquities dealer named Tsang Kwan.

The Hong Kong police arranged a video interview with Kwan for Adriana. He spoke fluent English, so they are able to communicate easily. She inquired about the specific dates of the payments in question. He promptly replied.

"Ah yes, these were purchased by Mr LeBlanc. An excellent customer."

"Do you have a record of what exactly he purchased?"

"Yes, and I'd be happy to provide you with the list."

When she received the list, she dived back into her research. Most of the items were Qin dynasty porcelain and silk, valued in the hundreds of thousands. The list went back several years, and the total value of the purchases was in the tens of millions.

The buyer was a French citizen from Lyon named Bruno LeBlanc. The French police told her that he had a record of assault, extortion and blackmail, but that he hadn't been seen in France for more than a decade. She contacted the Hong Kong police and asked them to investigate the address the items had been sent to, but all they found was an empty warehouse. Witnesses nearby had no information.

When she began searching for items that matched the descriptions of those purchased by LeBlanc, she found several silk tapestries in an auction manifest from Geneva. She contacted the Swiss police and the auction house and asked for information on the seller of the items.

The items had been sold by a French company called CoteBleue, which owned several casinos and nightclubs in Southern France. She discovered that CoteBleue was a subsidiary of an Estonian holding company called Solid Ventures, which in turn was owned by a Cayman Islands-based company registered to Bruno Leblanc.

The trail led directly back to him. It appeared that he was using antiquities to launder the profits from the human trafficking operations into his casinos in France. Due to the anonymous nature of the cryptocurrencies, though, they could not prove a direct link between LeBlanc and the human trafficking. To issue a warrant, they needed proof that he had access to the wallets associated with the Hong Kong exchange.

She checked the international immigration database and found that Leblanc was currently residing in Tugluavu, a small island country in the South Pacific.

Tugluavu had suffered from chronic instability, experiencing 14 coups d'état in the 50 years since its independence. Adriana contacted Tugluavan law enforcement, but when she explained the nature of the investigation, the chief of the Tugluavan police simply replied, "We have no cryptocurrency crime here," and abruptly ended the call.

Adriana was despondent. She went to Silvio to discuss possible options.

"It doesn't look like the Tugluavan authorities are interested in helping us with the investigation. It's a dead end," he said.

"We can't just give up. This is too big," Adriana replied.

"It's outside our jurisdiction."

"Is Tugluavu party to the international treaty on cryptocurrency crime?" Adriana asked.

"They're one of a dozen countries that didn't sign." They sat together in silence for a moment. After what she had seen from this gang, dropping the investigation was a bitter pill to swallow. Suddenly, Adriana's face lit up.

"Well, I've got two weeks of paid leave. Maybe I'll spend it on Tugluavu."

Silvio was shocked.

"Adriana, I know you put a lot of work into this, and it means a lot to you, but this is beyond our reach. Maybe some more evidence will appear. We'll just have to wait."

Adriana was becoming more animated. "Every day that this gang is operating, more people are killed and more girls victimised. When I'm on the job, you're the boss. But I get to decide what I do on my vacation. Don't worry, I won't break any laws."

Silvio was speechless, but he couldn't help but laugh.

Two days later, she boarded her flight for Port Suku'loa, the capital of Tugluavu.

The airport was in a state of chaos. Cats and chickens ran through the terminal, searching for scraps. When she collected her luggage, a crowd of men gathered around her offering to carry her bag for some change. She refused them politely and hailed a taxi, which took her along the pothole-filled road to her hotel.

Port Suku'loa was not a large city, and it soon became clear what was going on. There were a few huge mansions, while the rest of the city was composed of small wooden shacks and shanties. Talking with some of the locals, she learned that the largest mansion belonged to LeBlanc, while most of the others belonged to officials, including the president, who were all on his payroll.

The president had come to power four years ago, just one year before the drafting of the international treaty on cryptocurrency crime. Around the same time, LeBlanc moved to the island.

Adriana was unsure how to proceed. Even if she could somehow get evidence against him, the Tugluavan authorities would never extradite him. Nor would they authorise any kind of investigation inside the country.

She phoned Silvio and explained the situation.

"I think we have enough evidence to get a warrant if we could only get Leblanc out of the country somehow," she said.

"Even if you arrest him," said Silvio, "we don't have enough to go on as is. We'd need to get some kind of supporting evidence during the arrest. I don't see how that's possible without the cooperation of the Tugluavan authorities."

"Based on the money flowing in, he's loaded with cash at all times. I doubt he would leave the keys to his cryptocurrency wallets alone with his servants," she said. Silvio paused for a moment.

"You know," he said, "we have an excellent relationship with the Japanese police. It's not that far away either. If we could just get him to Japan somehow, I'm sure the Japanese would help us – but how? He knows he's safe there."

"I'll think about it and see if I can come up with something. Thanks, Silvio," she said and hung up.

She spent the rest of the day with her taxi driver, travelling around the city and asking questions. From several locals, she learned that Leblanc was an avid Olympique Lyonnais fan and would sometimes watch matches at the terrace bar of the Suku'loa Intercontinental, the island's premier hotel. She also learned that he had quite an appetite for women and could be seen with a different woman almost every week.

A plan began to form in her mind. Olympique Lyonnais were playing Juventus in two days, so she decided to try to meet him. She went to the island's best tailor, showed him a picture of a new Christian Dior dress and asked him if he could make a copy.

"Yes, I suppose I can do it. It'll cost three hundred shillings and be ready next week," he said.

"I don't have until next week. I need it by Friday."

"I'm sorry, but...."

"Can you do it for a thousand shillings?"

"I'd have to stay up all night working on it. Make it two thousand, and you have a deal."

It was a gamble, but she agreed. If it didn't work out, she might find some other occasion to use the dress, she thought.

She was usually so focused on work that she didn't pay much attention to her looks. She kept her hair in a simple ponytail, but that night she spent the rest of the evening watching video tutorials on how to put your hair into a herringbone braid. She received the finished evening dress the next day and completed her ensemble with some dark red lipstick. All of this was very out of character for her, but she was determined to try.

Shortly before the match, she entered the bar and ordered a drink. It seemed her outfit was working – the eyes of every man in the room swivelled to follow her as she walked across the terrace. It wasn't long before Leblanc swaggered in accompanied by two large bodyguards.

As he sat at his table, she briefly made eye contact and then, playing coy, immediately looked away. She then pretended to be busy with her phone. As the halftime whistle blew, it became clear her plan had worked.

"What's a beautiful girl like you doing in a place like this?" Leblanc asked.

She looked up from her phone. He had short blonde hair, no neck to speak of, and a nose that had apparently been broken several times. She felt a mixture of nausea and rage, both at the crimes she knew he was involved in and at the way he spoke to her.

But she put on a charming mask and began to chat with him. She told him she was here to do some research for a social development program. She accepted his offer of a drink and joined him at his table. She was relieved when he didn't ask her any questions about her work – instead, he started showing her photographs of his car collection.

Pretending to be interested, she struggled to laugh at his awful jokes. At one point, he leaned in to kiss her, but she turned away.

"I'm sorry. You're very nice, but it's just, I'm with someone."

"What does he have that I don't?" he replied angrily.

"Oh, nothing really. It's just that I don't want to be unfaithful."

"Why don't you come back to my house and we can discuss it more?" he asked, rather aggressively.

"Well, really, I'd love to, but maybe some other time."

He asked for her phone number; she gave it to him and left the bar.

The plan worked perfectly. As soon as she got back to her hotel, he began to message her, telling her what a mistake she'd made and how he could show her the best time of her life. His manner of speech was quite lewd as he described exactly *how* he wanted to show her the best time of her life, which made her all the more eager to see him locked up.

She flew to Tokyo the next day and met with the Japanese police, who had already been briefed by Silvio. They were in the process of issuing a warrant for LeBlanc. Meanwhile, she texted with Leblanc throughout the day. She told him she was back at her office but couldn't stop thinking about him, and how she regretted not going back to his house, and how she thought she would have to tell her boyfriend she'd met someone better.

She said she was wild with desire for him and couldn't wait another day. He fell into the trap and offered to visit her. He booked a flight to Tokyo, and she arranged to meet him at his hotel. As soon as he'd made his reservation, the police sprang into action and bugged his room.

When he arrived, Adriana told him she'd be there in a few hours and to make himself comfortable while she got herself ready. She waited with the police in a makeshift operations area set up in a neighbouring room. On the monitor screen, Leblanc paced the floor impatiently, dressed in his underwear. He paused occasionally to flex his muscles in the mirror. Finally, he sat down at his laptop and started to work.

The commander gave the order, and eight officers standing by across the corridor broke down Leblanc's door. Weapons drawn, they ordered him to lie face down on the floor. Before the suspect could make a move, an officer rushed forward and grabbed the still-open laptop from the arm of the settee, took it straight downstairs to a waiting squad car and sped to the police station.

At the station, Adriana began sorting through the files. They found a vast trove of information, including the keys to the wallets that linked Leblanc to his gang. Based on their findings, they contacted law enforcement across Europe, Asia, and South America. In the following days, dozens of houses were raided 16 countries, and hundreds of girls were freed.

Back in Sao Paulo, Adriana told her story to Silvio and the team at the FAC, and they celebrated her success. But the next day, she was back at her desk. Cryptocurrency had changed the way criminals worked – the police would have to adapt to that, but they still had a long way to go. Until human nature changed, Adriana thought, she would have plenty to keep her busy.

***

Caveat Emptor

An Introduction to the World of Cryptocurrency Fraud

Although the currency of choice for criminals is still, by a wide margin, the US dollar, a great deal of media coverage has associated cryptocurrency with money laundering, drug dealing, and even terrorism. These issues are relatively minor compared to the biggest crime-related problem associated with cryptocurrency – fraud.

When Adriana shifted from fighting counterfeiting to cryptocurrency crimes, the first problem she encountered was the issue of fraud. This is by no means fiction; rather, it's a reality that police agencies and governments around the world are struggling with. The ability to send money anonymously over the internet has empowered a wide range of criminals. This section brings the reader up to speed on the nature and variety of cryptocurrency fraud. To truly understand this issue, however, it's necessary to dive into some of the internal dynamics of the cryptocurrency ecosystem, including the many cryptocurrencies that have emerged since the development of Bitcoin.

Altcoins 101

Not long after Bitcoin was born, copycats began to appear. This is not surprising; all you have to do to create a copy of the Bitcoin network is copy and paste the code and make a few changes.

The first few copies tried modifying certain parameters: faster confirmation times, different mining algorithms – some even proposed using mining to discover new prime numbers. Most of these new currencies claimed to be superior to Bitcoin in some way, or at least to serve some need that Bitcoin didn't.

Privacy Coins

Privacy coins are coins that claim to have superior properties of anonymity and confidentiality. All Bitcoin transactions are public, so some claim that these coins offer better protection against invasions of privacy. Critics argue that these coins can enable criminals, as described in the story of Adriana.

Examples of privacy coins include Monero, Dash, Zcash, and Verge.

Smart Contract Platforms

Smart contract platforms are distributed networks that allow executable programs to be stored on their blockchains. These include networks like Ethereum, NEO, EOS, Ark, Lisk, and Tron. Each of these networks has a native currency whose value is derived from the notion that users will need the currency to use the network in the future.

ICOs

ICO stands for *initial coin offering*. Similar to an initial public offering (IPO) of a stock, an ICO is a fundraising initiative in which digital shares or tokens are issued on top of a blockchain. Many ICOs have proved to be fraudulent and ended in failure, largely because they are relatively easy to create.

Settlement Networks

Settlement networks are networks that respond mainly to the criticism that Bitcoin is too slow and its transaction fees are too high. The main players in this space include Ripple and Stellar. These are not conventional blockchains but rather are designed to be used by banks and other institutional actors for increased efficiency in international settlements.

These networks have been criticised for their centralised nature. In the case of both Ripple and Stellar, the issuance of the currency is controlled by centralised organisations who control the entire supply of the coins, in contrast to Bitcoin's decentralised distribution model and guaranteed scarcity.

Stablecoins

Stablecoins are designed to address Bitcoin's volatility. These are cryptocurrencies that are tied to assets that are more stable in exchange rate than Bitcoin – usually major currencies like US dollars or stable assets like gold. They are often guaranteed by an institution that claims to back up the value of the coins with reserves.

Stablecoins allow many applications that are difficult with Bitcoin due to its relative volatility. They have been criticised for being centralised and requiring trust in the organisation that issues them, and some stablecoin custodians have been notorious for refusing audits.

Not all of the many cryptocurrencies created after Bitcoin are scams, but they lend themselves very well to scams. The rapid growth of the cryptocurrency space and the technical complexity of the subject mean that investors are not well-positioned to distinguish genuine projects from scams. Even the developers of projects themselves don't always know if their project is viable or not.

One of the most common cryptocurrency scams is the *pump-and-dump*.

The Pump-and-Dump

The unregulated nature of the cryptocurrency industry has led to the rise of many pump-and-dump schemes. In these schemes, a crypto asset or token is promoted as having revolutionary potential, thus inflating investor expectations.

In reality, there is little real value in the underlying asset, but marketing smoke and mirrors, as well as market manipulation, inflate the price, thus luring unsuspecting investors into putting their money in. This is the *pump*. Soon after, the architects of the scheme *dump* their holdings of the asset, taking the investments and leaving the investors with nothing of value.

Some of these schemes are implemented by the developers of a project, but bad outside actors can also pump a legitimate project after buying up coins or tokens that represent that project. Once they drive up interest through marketing campaigns, they then dump their coins or tokens at a much higher price than they bought them for, crashing the market in the process and disappearing with the money.

These kinds of schemes have been present in stock markets around the world for ages, so blame can't really be placed on new technology.

For example, one of the most famous historical instances of investment fraud was the South Sea Bubble of the early 18th century. The South Sea Company was originally conceived as a method to consolidate and pay off British debt by means of a monopoly on trade in the South Pacific.

On the surface, this sounded like a fine plan – and indeed, at the time, many fortunes were made in similar ventures. But these expectations were blown out of proportion by unscrupulous behaviour and dishonesty on the part of the company's architects. The managers of the company bribed politicians to pass Acts of Parliament to facilitate their scheme and used the company's funds to purchase shares and drive up prices. Money was borrowed using company shares as collateral in order to buy more shares. Prices went sky high.

The only problem was that the area was under the control of the Spanish, and the British didn't control any trade in the South Sea at that time. The managers of the company took their profits, and thousands of investors were ruined as share prices collapsed. The company went bankrupt without ever generating any real profits.

So these types of scams are clearly much older than cryptocurrency. But incidents like the South Sea bubble are also the reason we have investor protection regulation today. But how do you enforce such regulations in the world's first truly global market?

The answer is that you can't, and that's actually alright. The agency described in Adriana's story is a possible alternative to our present regime. It's quite understandable that when people get swindled, they go running to the government asking for assistance. But is that sufficient justification for banning everyone else from certain activities on the grounds of protecting the public?

Certainly, to protect the public from fraud is a noble aim, but providing that protection requires power, and that power can be abused. Ultimately, preventing fraud, particularly when it comes to technology investments, must rely on education. There has always been a strong argument for relying on personal responsibility rather than government controls. Those who prefer to have guidance from governments should have the option – such an option was described in Adriana's story in the form of the International Cryptocurrency Fraud Prevention Committee.

This could go a long way towards preventing unsuspecting investors from losing funds in risky investments. At the same time, such a policy option would not prevent well-informed retail investors from participating in markets.

Ponzi Schemes

Another common scam is the Ponzi scheme. In this variant, investors pay in money and receive spectacular returns in a short span of time. When word gets out, more people invest, and the scheme grows. The orchestrators of the scam are not actually investing the money, however, but instead are paying out the profits using the funds paid in by new investors. When the scheme stops growing, they are no longer able to pay the promised returns, and the entire thing collapses. In most cases, the later investors lose all their money, while the earlier ones sometimes make good earnings.

If a project is paying out guaranteed returns in excess of 50-100% annual return on investment, there's a good chance you may be dealing with a Ponzi scheme.

Vaporware

Vaporware generally refers to a type of software marketed and sold before it is actually functional. A wide array of fabulous-sounding concepts have been marketed within cryptocurrency markets. Some of these concepts were impossible, and the people collecting funds to develop them knew it. In other cases, well-intentioned developers dearly want a concept to be viable, but it simply isn't.

Ethereum is frequently accused of being vapourware by Bitcoin maximalists, a term used to designate people who believe Bitcoin is the one and only worthwhile cryptocurrency. This accusation is based on the fact that Ethereum achieved a very high valuation based on speculation about possible future uses. Ethereum has also been subject to several major hacks that have led some to criticise it for being marketed as a functional network when, in reality, it is still in the experimental phase.

Giveaway Scams

Giveaway scams usually involve promises of doubling your money in the space of a few days or weeks. You are asked to send some Bitcoin or another currency to a given address and promised that you will receive the money back, plus profit, at a date in the near future. Of course, if it looks too good to be true, it usually is, and once you send it, the money's gone forever.

These scams often try to cash in on the social credibility of prominent figures by impersonating their social media accounts. In July 2020, a group of hackers took over the Twitter accounts of several such celebrities, including Elon Musk, Bill Gates, Barack Obama, Joe Biden, and Jeff Bezos, and promised to double the value of Bitcoin that people sent to a bogus address. In this way, they managed to collect Bitcoin worth approximately $280,000 at the time.

Fear, Uncertainty, and Doubt

Fear, uncertainty, and doubt (often abbreviated as FUD) describe a situation where someone has an interest in lowering the value of a cryptocurrency. One of the most common reasons someone would use FUD is to cause uninformed investors to panic sell at a price lower than the actual value.

FUD is often spread by rumours, sometimes in waves by large numbers of fake, online personas.

Ransomware

Although this is not technically a scam, ransomware is a growing threat that is worth mentioning in any discussion of cryptocurrency-related crime. Ransomware is delivered by a computer virus that infiltrates a victim's computer or network.

It then encrypts the data, rendering the system unusable, and displays a message demanding a ransom, usually in Bitcoin, in exchange for the decryption key.

A newer variant on this is not only to encrypt data but also to steal sensitive data and threaten to release it to the public if the ransom is not paid.

Some of the gangs conducting these kinds of attacks may have some political backing. For example, the REvil gang, also known as Sodinokibi, uses viruses whose code prevents the virus from being used inside Russia, the former Soviet states, or Iran. Instead, the attacks tend to focus on the Russian government's rivals, mainly in the West. Other attacks have been detected originating from North Korea.

This is another good piece of evidence illustrating that not all cryptocurrency crime problems will have law enforcement solutions because they may enter into the realm of politics. This also illustrates the futility of trying to ban or illegalise cryptocurrencies, which are not going to go away. This is a new reality from which there is no escaping, and the sooner we come to terms with it, the better prepared we will be for the changes ahead.

Ethereum and Smart Contracts

While some consider Ethereum to be a scam, many other sincere individuals genuinely believe in the potential of the technology, and Ethereum has already been deployed in a limited way in certain novel use cases. Nobody denies, however, that Ethereum has enabled a large number of scams. To understand why and to have a well-rounded understanding of the cryptocurrency ecosystem, it's important to understand what Ethereum is, how it works, and why it's important.

Early on in Bitcoin's life, when people realised that any type of text could be immutably stored on the blockchain, discussions began about including computer code. Ethereum was originally born from a proposal to expand the amount of data that could be contained in Bitcoin transactions. Bitcoin has a feature called OP_RETURN that allows additional data to be included with transactions. Expanding it, some argued, could allow the creation of "smart contracts".

This would have very powerful consequences. For example, consider buying a car. You could simply program a transaction to say, "If Alice sends 10,000 to Bob, then transfer the vehicle registration certificate from Bob to Alice." In this way, the need for a government agency to maintain ownership records is eliminated entirely, much as Bitcoin eliminates the need for a custodian to maintain bank balances.

This is just one of many applications. While Bitcoin enabled decentralised monetary transfers, smart contracts on a blockchain could offer decentralised loans, crowdfunding, notarisation, and many other functions. This could theoretically save huge amounts of legal busywork and lead to massive efficiency gains in a wide range of governmental and corporate applications.

The Bitcoin community rejected the proposal over concerns about centralisation, arguing that if the blockchain contained more data, it would become increasingly difficult for ordinary people to store a copy, and the network would fall into the hands of fewer and fewer individuals. This centralisation would ultimately defeat the original object of Bitcoin by exposing the network to the possibility of becoming a government or private monopoly.

So, a group of programmers who believed in the idea crowdfunded several million dollars' worth of Bitcoin and set to work developing the completely independent Ethereum network.

The stated aim of Ethereum was to be a *world computer*. Instead of only verifying transactions, like Bitcoin, Ethereum would allow the deployment of decentralised applications, or dapps, running off of code stored on the Ethereum network rather than in the hard drives of individual devices.

And instead of serving as digital gold like Bitcoin, Ethereum's native currency, ether, would be used as *gas* to power operations on the Ethereum network. This was a different value proposition than Bitcoin, so demand would be generated by users wishing to run operations on the network. If Ethereum was able to deliver on its incredible promises, it might mean that ether could one day be tremendously valuable. And thus, a speculative frenzy began.

Smart contracts on Ethereum made it very easy for anyone to create their own coin.

Cryptocurrencies are ultimately based on programs, and since Ethereum allowed these programs to be stored on the blockchain, anyone could publish a program that established the existence of a provably scarce asset: tokens. These tokens led to the ICO craze. Many investors saw the fortunes that were made with Bitcoin and were keen to catch "the next Bitcoin". This and the international nature of a fully online market was fertile ground for dishonest players and led to a huge increase in cryptocurrency scams – clearly demonstrating why financial regulations were introduced in the first place.

One of the main criticisms of the Ethereum community is what many people see as the exaggerated claims made by some of its members about the network's potential. While these claims may have some validity, many of the underlying assumptions have yet to be adequately tested. Bitcoin, on the other hand, does nothing more or less than what it claims to do.

Of course, this is the nature of investing in technological development. Most tech startups fail in their initial aims. But in the case of Ethereum, ICOs provided legitimate developers and researchers, as well as criminals, with a very powerful tool for raising funds.

There has since been a legal backlash in many countries, with several banning ICO's outright after citizens lost large sums of money.

Consensus Mechanisms: More than Just Technology

Many cryptocurrency scams were pushed on the basis of technical superiority. The promoters argued that their coins were vastly superior to Bitcoin or Ethereum and thereby tried to drive up speculative interest. But there's much more to cryptocurrencies than technical considerations.

Network participants reach agreement by means of a consensus mechanism. So far, this book has only discussed proof-of-work, which is the consensus mechanism for Bitcoin and most of the other major cryptocurrencies. As Bitcoin has grown from the fringe hobby of a few hackers to a global force, an array of alternative consensus mechanisms have emerged.

Proof of stake was one of the first, but there are many others, including proof-of-time-elapsed, proof-of-importance, proof-of-reputation, Byzantine fault tolerance, and decentralised acyclic graphs (DAG) based consensus. This is quite a technical field, encompassing computer science, economics, cryptography, game theory, and a number of other fields.

Confusing matters further is the fact that cryptocurrency enables direct monetisation of the *perception* of technical superiority. Many teams would like to convince investors to move their money out of Bitcoin and into their project, so you can find many "Bitcoin killers" out there claiming to be light years ahead of Bitcoin's antiquated technology.

This was most visible in the second half of 2017, when a surge among alternative cryptocurrencies briefly took over more than half of the total cryptocurrency market. After this brief surge, the speculative craze subsided, and Bitcoin returned to dominating over 70% of the total global cryptocurrencies market.

Bitcoin's popularity remains steady despite numerous claims of technological superiority from a range of other coins. Bitcoin maintains its position because the challenges made against it are not technical but ideological.

A cryptocurrency is not a business, a network, or a government. However, it mixes elements of all three. With stocks, you have established metrics for assessing value – assets, liabilities, revenue, and so forth. But with cryptocurrencies, much of their value is based on prospective future adoption, which is much harder to assess.

The calculations people make when choosing a cryptocurrency have a lot to do with politics. Bitcoin has been an ideological project from the very beginning. This differentiates it from other technological shifts, like the development of the telegram, automobile, or steam engine. What determines the success of a cryptocurrency, more than its cost or overall efficiency, is how well it addresses political and moral concerns.

Crucial to all of this is centralisation. If too much of the Bitcoin network falls into the hands of a single party, the potential exists to attack the network and double-spend funds, thus reducing confidence and the value of the network. It also renders it more vulnerable to attacks from hostile governments. So, many Bitcoin advocates are more than willing to tolerate a technology that performs less than perfectly if it addresses their political concerns.

Another major ideological issue is environmentalism (more about this in the next chapter). On environmental matters, Ethereum developers, for example, tend to have a different perspective than Bitcoin supporters and, as such, take issue with Bitcoin mining because it consumes large amounts of energy. For this reason, the Ethereum network has gradually transitioned to proof-of-stake, a consensus method that consumes less energy but raises a number of concerns about long-term centralisation.

The importance of both technological and ideological decisions in the development of decentralised networks means that there can be a lot of conflict within the communities of developers that build these networks. After all, there is no management or boss to take the final decision. This also leads to issues with scams because anyone can split away from a network while claiming to be the "real" network in a process called a *fork*.

Fork Me? No, Fork You!

Decentralised networks are very difficult, if not impossible, to destroy. However, this also makes them very difficult to govern effectively. Cryptocurrency networks are a collection of nodes communicating with each other. If they are not running *exactly* the same software, they will not accept communications from other nodes.

This is why there will only ever be 21 million Bitcoins. If you are part of the Bitcoin network, you are welcome to modify your software and change 21 million to 22 million, but by doing so, you will cut yourself off, and all of the coins you mine will only be considered valid in your own little network. Of course, if you could convince others to join you, then your coins might actually have some value. That's for the market to decide.

When a person or group running cryptocurrency software decides to change some aspect of the software, a *fork* occurs. This means that the network essentially splits like a fork in the road. There are two types of forks – soft forks and hard forks. A soft fork usually means minor changes are made, such that the nodes running the modified software can still communicate with the main network. A hard fork, on the other hand, means that the forked software is no longer compatible with other versions of the software.

If a hard fork is unanimously adopted by the operators of a network, there is no split in the community. Bitcoin has gone through a number of hard forks, and some have been highly contentious. Much of this debate centred on concerns of centralisation. The most notable was the fork surrounding the SegWit debates.

SegWit is an abbreviation of "segregated witness", which was a proposal to allow Bitcoin to process more transactions. As the network began to gain popularity, blocks filled up too quickly with transactions, leading to long wait times. One proposal to solve this issue was to increase the block size, which had been capped at 1 MB.

Factions formed, with some arguing that larger blocks would make it harder for small operators to keep a copy of the entire blockchain. According to this faction, limiting the verification of transactions only to people with expensive, specialised equipment would compromise the principle of decentralisation. And if the network became centralised, it could be subject to manipulation by those in control or could be shut down by any hostile government or regime.

On the other hand, with small blocks, transaction fees would increase, which would mean that Bitcoin would become less and less suitable for day-to-day purchases. The result was a fork, which led to the network dividing into Bitcoin Core and Bitcoin Cash. Both claimed to be the real Bitcoin, and all eyes were on the miners to see which direction they would choose. Ultimately, the bulk of the network and the market sided with Bitcoin Core. Hence, Bitcoin Cash became a fork in the main Bitcoin network.

The DAO and the Ethereum Classic Fork

Since the Ethereum network tries to do much more than the Bitcoin network, much more can go wrong with it. Apart from allowing a change in the underlying program that a network runs on, a hard fork enables the blockchain to be changed. When an experimental smart contract was hacked, resulting in the loss of millions of dollars' worth of Ethereum, the Ethereum community decided to use a hard fork to "reverse" the theft.

There was a broad but not total consensus on this course of action. Some community members felt it would set a bad precedent since immutability was one of the main aims of the project.

In the end, the majority backed the fork, and only a small fraction of dissenters remained on the original Ethereum blockchain, which was rebranded Ethereum Classic. Many boycotted Ethereum Classic because using it would be a form of support for the hacker.

This goes very much against the ethos of tamper resistance that characterises Bitcoin, and to some extent, this is necessary with an experimental project like Ethereum. In any case, this demonstrates an interesting aspect of blockchains when it comes to crime and theft. While many see the ability to change the blockchain as a fatal flaw, others see it as an effective means of securing against catastrophic loss. This is especially important when dealing with a more complex system, like Ethereum, with many more possible attack vectors.

DeFi and the Limits of Blockchains

While the ICO craze peaked in 2017, more recently, there has been a second-wave speculative craze centred on the Ethereum ecosystem. Referred to as "decentralised finance" or DeFi for short, this trend can be viewed as a continuation of the ICO craze.

One of the first projects in this space was Maker's Dai, the first successful decentralised stablecoin. The Dai uses smart contracts and incentives to issue fully collateralised stablecoins whose value is pegged to the dollar. This development came in response to criticism of the world's largest stablecoins, Tether's USDT. Tether was accused of not fully collateralising their coins, or in other words, doing exactly what the banks do all the time.

This behaviour is exactly what cryptocurrency was designed to get away from, so there's a strong demand for it. The only trouble with the Dai is that being collateralised with cryptocurrency, it needs much higher levels of collateral to compensate for the volatility. In other words, imagine that you deposit $2,000 of Ethereum's native currency, ether, into a smart contract in order to get $1,000 worth of Dai. This ends up being used primarily for gambling on future price movements by borrowing against cryptocurrency.

While this may have its place, unfortunately, DeFi projects aim primarily to replace functions of the existing financial system without changing it all that much. The idea is to make the financial system more efficient by automating functions that would ordinarily require public trust in the bank or financial institution. In many cases, however, this means trusting in code, which is written by humans, who make mistakes.

Although DeFi was very hot in 2020, announcements of hacks or scams were an almost weekly event in which either code failed, resulting in investor losses; or some other breach of trust occurred. For example, in March of 2020, a major swing in the price of Ethereum resulted in the loss of millions of dollars for people who'd put money into the Maker DAO, the smart contract which issues Dai.

Since the Maker DAO stabilises the price of the Dai by liquidating collateral, several market participants were able to purchase this collateral at severely discounted rates. Technically, this is not a hack, or theft, or fraud; nonetheless, it resulted in the loss of approximately $9 million worth of ether. In response, the victims filed a class-action lawsuit against the Maker Foundation, which developed the Maker DAO.

In February, a margin lending program called bZx lost over a million dollars in user funds, not due to a hack but by manipulating asset prices to trick the program into giving out larger loans than would ordinarily be allowed. In April, a hacker took $25 million from a Chinese lending platform called Lend.me using the same vulnerability that caused the original DAO hack. In September, the managers of a liquidity mining platform called YFDEX disappeared with $25 million in investors' funds. In October, a yield aggregator called Harvest lost $25 million in the hack of a smart contract. In November, SharkTron, a DeFi platform associated with the cryptocurrency Tron, lost huge amounts in a hack.

Much of the movement behind DeFi is grounded in a vision of *code as law*, in which programmers design the governmental systems of the future. Unfortunately, it seems that programmers are just as likely to be incompetent as bankers.

One could argue that all these hacks and scams are just growing pains. After all, many planes crashed during the pioneering days of aviation. One of the problems with this narrative is the actual goal of most DeFi projects. In many cases, they are replicating exotic financial instruments like derivatives, options and swaps, which are integral to the swindling and deception that conventional financial markets currently engage in.

The reality of the modern financial system is that complicated terminology and legal arrangements are used to mask what is, in fact, simple swindling. Wealth is created without creating any actual value. In many or most cases, DeFi projects are attempting to replicate these same processes in a decentralised manner.

Another problem with the hype surrounding decentralised systems is that, in many ways, they are much less efficient than centralised systems. A blockchain's security is derived from having many independent nodes maintaining copies of the blockchain, ensuring that data cannot be modified. To propagate data within the network, it must be included in a block, which means fees need to be paid.

For this reason, programs based on blockchains are much more expensive than centralised programs. The only real reason a blockchain should be used is if it absolutely *must* be used. It's very unlikely, as some people imagine, that blockchains will ever be able to replace *all* centralised systems because centralised databases are vastly more efficient and cost-effective than blockchains.

Furthermore, consider, for example, a decentralised Airbnb. On the surface, this sounds like a good idea. Airbnb takes administrative fees of around three per cent of every booking. With a fully automated, decentralised system, this fee could be reduced to a fraction of that.

The problem with this is that many essential functions cannot be automated. For example, dispute resolution, investigating insurance claims, processing refunds, and other activities all fall under the responsibility of Airbnb's administrators.

For this reason, Bitcoin proponents argue that Bitcoin's simplicity is actually an advantage rather than a sign of inferior technology.

Bitcoin has a more or less perfect record when it comes to hacks, though many companies dealing with Bitcoin have been hacked. Bitcoin proponents argue the Bitcoin will form the bedrock of a new financial system, and so far, its track record supports this vision.

By contrast, both the ICO craze and DeFi hype share a wave of wildly inflated expectations about the potential of the technology, driving a speculative frenzy in which very little value is actually created. Some gems may emerge from this madness, much as Google, Amazon, and Facebook emerged from the madness of the dot-com bubble. For the time being, however, the cryptocurrency market remains much more dangerous than the early internet bubble because of the ease of transacting anonymously and the unregulated nature of the space.

As with any gold rush, some individuals get lucky and become very rich. A smaller number find wealth through careful deliberation and wise investment. These successful investors are outnumbered by a wide margin by thousands upon thousands of investors who were lured by the promise of easy wealth and lost huge sums of money in the process.

Black Markets, Grey Markets

With the rise of cryptocurrency, dark web marketplaces are also on the rise. On these anonymous, online marketplaces, it's possible to buy anything from heroin to handguns, and you can even hire hitmen and hackers (although most or all of the online assassins for hire are actually scammers). The overwhelming majority of the use of cryptocurrency on the dark web is for the purchase of drugs.

In the case of illegal drug trafficking, we also have to ask why exactly is the market for illegal drugs so big in the first place? Decades of the *war on drugs* and billions of dollars spent on arresting and imprisoning drug pushers and smugglers has utterly failed to stop the trade in illegal drugs. Perhaps it's time to consider different strategies.

While there is no doubt that much harm results from drug abuse, does it automatically follow that every dark web transaction is bad? The fact is that many bad laws exist all across the world, and just because something is illegal does not always mean it is immoral. Many situations lie in legal grey areas.

In the United States, for example, there was a scandal recently surrounding the Epinephrine auto-injector, which is a medical device used for treating anaphylactic shock. Many children with severe food allergies keep these devices with them at all times in case they are accidentally exposed to an allergen, and the injectors have saved many lives.

In the UK, they cost the NHS about £48 to make available to the public, who can purchase them for about £8.50. They were also relatively inexpensive in the US until a few years ago. One of the producers of these products in the US market went out of business in 2015, and another generic competitor was denied a licence to produce the drug in 2016, leaving only one company with market dominance.

They used their monopoly on the market to increase the price of the device by over 500% to $600. As a result, many parents could not afford them, and the lives of thousands of children were put at risk for the sake of corporate greed.

Technically speaking, it would be illegal for these parents to buy these devices online. They require a prescription in the US, although they are sold over the counter in most other countries. And yet, in this situation, a dark marketplace could serve to correct a serious failure in health regulation.

There are many such drugs available on dark web marketplaces, and it's very unreasonable to expect people not to take matters into their own hands when their national health care system fails them. In cases of severe corruption, the price of a drug could even be inflated by collusion between private companies and regulators. In such a case, citizens could risk legal repercussions for exercising what in the rest of the world is considered a basic right.

Even when it comes to illegal drugs, there are ways that dark marketplaces can actually reduce the overall harm done to addicts. Online drug dealers have to rely on their reputation because their customers can leave reviews in the same way buyers on Amazon or eBay do.

Sink or Swim

Rising to the Challenge of a New Financial Paradigm

Cryptocurrency is a revolutionary technology, but it is not a fix for human nature. For the entirety of human history, there have always been individuals who are willing to harm others for the sake of personal gain. Technology changes the ways that both criminals and police work, but the underlying principles remain surprisingly stable through the course of technological revolutions.

With every technological paradigm shift, many problems are solved, but new challenges arise. In the industrial revolution, major gains in standards of living and productivity were realised, but the use of coal led to environmental and health concerns. With the rise of the automobile, there was an increase in fatal road accidents. Likewise, with Bitcoin and cryptocurrency come new challenges.

There is no shortage of voices speaking out against cryptocurrency. Benoît Cœuré, a member of the Executive Board of the European Central Bank, went as far as to call Bitcoin "the evil spawn of the financial crisis". Bill Harris, the CEO of PayPal, wrote an article titled "Bitcoin is the greatest scam in history". JP Morgan CEO Jamie Dimon insulted Bitcoiners, saying, "If you're stupid enough to buy it, you'll one day pay the price."

But all of these voices have one thing in common. They are all in prominent positions at the head of institutions that are directly threatened by open, free finance.

There are so many vested interests in the financial industry that it's very difficult to paint an accurate picture of the true impact of the technology. As described in the previous chapters, cryptocurrency has the very real potential to put a number of very powerful individuals quite literally out of work. It's easy for those who feel threatened by Bitcoin and cryptocurrency to distort its image by focusing on negative aspects while ignoring the positive. Likewise, those who have vested interests in cryptocurrency's success sometimes overlook the negative points.

It's important to keep this in mind when we hear condemnation of the role of cryptocurrency in facilitating criminal activity.

We need to be aware of the challenges that the technology will pose to law enforcement and security. At the same time, it's equally important to be aware of how it can be used to fight crime. Cryptocurrency is simply a tool – and it can be used for good or evil. Some types of crime can be drastically reduced by cryptocurrency. Counterfeiting can be entirely eliminated, freeing up critical police resources. The higher level of security associated with cryptocurrencies can also dramatically reduce credit card fraud, which presently causes billions worth of damage every year.

Some types of crime will decline as a result of cryptocurrency, while other types may be enabled. In any case, however we feel about it, cryptocurrency is here to stay. No force on earth can eliminate cryptocurrency outright, nor should anyone want to, given how much the technology has to offer. The sooner we come to terms with this reality, the sooner we can develop new methods of fighting crime and adapt.

Adriana's story illustrates the critical need to attack the root causes of crime rather than only the symptoms. Law enforcement is absolutely necessary for maintaining social order and peace, but in many cases, crime is a symptom of broader social issues. For example, in the case of cryptocurrency-related fraud, effective education on the nature of blockchain technology can be a much more effective means of preventing damage than only prosecuting fraudsters.

That Bruno LeBlanc was able to bribe the government of an impoverished country into protecting his operation highlights this point – law enforcement cannot overcome political problems on the international level. Police forces must shift their focus from catching criminals toward protecting citizens.

As other forms of crime are decreasing in the 21st century, cybercrime is on the rise. And many of these crimes are not due to technical failures but social ones.

The first line of defence against these kinds of crimes is not to be found in surveillance and spying on the populations of entire countries. This breeds an atmosphere of mistrust between governments and their citizens and sacrifices the fundamental right to privacy for the sake of security. Rather, citizens must be equipped with the knowledge to protect themselves against fraud and crime. This requires broad-based, educational initiatives to teach people how to protect themselves from crime and take more responsibility for themselves. While the money spent trying to catch criminals only has a momentary effect, the money invested in education can yield dividends for generations.

Other major causes of crime are economic inequality and lack of opportunity. Throughout this book, you will find examples of ways in which cryptocurrency can address problems of economic inequality. Even the problem of human trafficking, mentioned in Adriana's story, is driven by a lack of economic opportunities. Many of the victims of human trafficking originate from economically disadvantaged backgrounds. Paedophiles are well known to travel to impoverished countries to take advantage of children, and many of the women coerced or forced into prostitution originate from poor backgrounds in Eastern Europe, Asia, and Africa. Focusing on bringing the advantages enabled by cryptocurrency to disadvantaged communities may be a much more effective means of fighting crime than law enforcement alone.

Rather than suppressing innovation, governments need to embrace the transformative effects of cryptocurrency and its potential to address the underlying causes of crime. Law enforcement is an important part of the equation, and more international cooperation and standards are certainly needed to control cryptocurrency-related crime in the short term. If we draft wise policy responses to the rise of cryptocurrency, however, it can serve as a powerful tool for reducing overall crime rates over the long term.

4. Yuri Vasiliyev

Powering Sustainability

Yuri wasn't disappointed with the way his life turned out, although it was not at all what he expected. After all, who would expect a computer scientist to end up as a strawberry farmer in Siberia? When he was at university, there weren't even any strawberry farms in Siberia. But things change, and sometimes you have to move with the times.

Yuri grew up in a small town in Western Russia, not far from Moscow. He was particularly gifted at mathematics and loved playing with computers from an early age. Out of high school, he received a scholarship to Moscow State University to study computer science. During his studies, he lived in the dormitories, where he shared a room with an eccentric engineering student called Dmitry. They sometimes stayed up late discussing every topic imaginable, from women and ice hockey to space travel and mycology. But somehow, conversations with Dmitry always came back to the same topic: the monetary system and the global banking cartel.

Dmitry was not the most fanatical conspiracy theorist in the world, but he certainly had a strong conspiratorial bent. Occasionally, he would go on about the Illuminati and their various plots for world domination. Yuri just had to roll his eyes, and Dmitry usually got the hint and quickly changed the subject. But occasionally, Dmitry's conspiratorial ramblings would make a little too much sense. He would drive his points home by showing Yuri YouTube videos detailing the Masonic symbolism on the US dollar and explaining how humanity was caught in a cycle of debt slavery.

Even if it was interesting to talk about, it seemed to Yuri these discussions were a waste of time. If there was something evil about the international banking system, there was nothing they could do about it anyway, he thought.

That changed one year in the dead of winter. It was two weeks before Christmas, and the two roommates were staying in the dorms to finish their term projects before going home to visit their families. An ageing pipe that transported heating water to their building burst, and the young men's flat quickly became intolerably cold.

They went to the library to work, expecting the pipe would be repaired by the time they got back. As it turned out, the person responsible for the repairs was on holiday. At the university's maintenance office, they got a lukewarm response from the indifferent staff. Instead of summoning a plumber, they suggested Yuri and Dmitry put on extra layers of clothing.

Having little choice, they took the advice, but even wrapped in three t-shirts, two sweaters, a jacket and two blankets, they still slept terribly. The two friends were shivering in front of the library when it opened at seven in the morning. They hurried in and made directly for the table next to the heater, relieved to be out of the cold.

Yuri could feel the lack of sleep was seriously affecting his powers of concentration. Stepping out for a cigarette break, he told Dmitry there was no way he could spend another night like that.

"I can't take this anymore. I'm going to have to buy an electric space heater."

"Don't do that," Dmitry said. "The heating will be back on in a few days. Don't waste your money."

"It's no good. I'm getting nothing done. I need to finish this project, and I keep nodding off. Even if it's only for one day, if it helps me finish the project, it'll worth it. Come on, why don't we pay half each? We can always resell it later."

"Who's going to buy an electric heater when they've already got gas? No, if you want it, you pay for it."

"Where do they even sell electric heaters?" Yuri wondered aloud.

Suddenly, Dmitry's face lit up.

"You know what? I've got an idea. A friend of mine's having trouble with his girlfriend."

"What's that got to do with my heater?" Yuri asked, flustered.

"He's mining Bitcoin in his flat, and his girlfriend's been complaining about the noise and the heat. She told him it's either her or the Bitcoin. It's a tough choice, but I think he's gonna go with the Bitcoin."

"You mean that 'magical' internet money?"

Dmitry launched into an excited monologue about how Bitcoin was going to free the world from financial slavery and how they could be part of the transformation. Yuri was more interested in heating the apartment with computers and making money at the same time. Dmitry insisted the heat generated would be enough to keep their flat comfortably warm, and the Bitcoin generated could be traded for real money, which they could then exchange for real beer.

Yuri's scholarship stipend was far from lavish, so this was enough to convince him. Dmitry's Bitcoin-mining friend, Anton, jumped at the chance of housing the miners elsewhere since it meant keeping his girlfriend. In exchange, Anton would give Yuri and Dmitry a percentage of the profits. His electricity savings would cover the roommates' share anyway, as electricity in student housing was free.

Dmitry was right: the moment the miners were up and running, the flat got warmer, so warm in fact that they had to open the windows. And although the whirring of the machines was quite noisy, they were so happy to be out of the cold that they hardly minded.

The next morning, Yuri's curiosity and his love of computers got the better of him, and he started to play around with the computer running the mining software. He wanted to see how much money they'd earned during the night but was also wondering how the software worked. He opened a console and checked the mining client's list of commands. He then accessed the hash function log and watched the stream of data flowing by.

It was fascinating. Somehow, these noisy computer chips were generating money and heating his room in the process. He forgot about his term project and spent hours reading about Bitcoin and studying the source code. On an internet forum, he came across the phrase *code as law*.

He'd never been interested in politics, but as a technology lover, he'd long been fascinated by science fiction stories that discussed handing over the functions of government to a supercomputer. And while he'd never experienced it himself, he'd heard his parents talking about the devaluation of the rouble, so he could certainly see a need to remove human error from the issuance of money.

As an engineer, he was also fascinated by the maths behind it. He realised that the chips were operating at below capacity, so he examined the firmware of the chips in the mining units and began making modifications to increase the output. He also realised there were some optimisations to be made to the operating system and made some changes there as well.

When Anton dropped by a few days later to see how everything was going, he was pleasantly surprised to find higher earnings than he'd expected.

"What did you do?" Anton asked. "This is great!"

"Nothing much. I just modified the firmware to optimise hash rate and cleaned up some of the processes in the kernel of the operating system." Yuri replied nonchalantly.

Anton was so impressed that he told one of his friends who then wanted Yuri to come and help him with his miners as well. Yuri was happy to oblige and soon found himself learning more and more about mining.

By the time summer arrived, however, the miners were turning their flat into a furnace. They called Anton and told him it was time to end their arrangement. Anton came over and pleaded with them.

"Please, I've got a plan. I just need one more week."

"Come on, man! It's like a *banya* in here!" Dmitry cried.

"Look, guys," Anton went on, "I'm on to something really big here. I've got an uncle in Yakutsk, and he works with a guy who's in charge of the hydroelectric dam there. We've finally got the director convinced, and we can get electricity for next to nothing." Dmitry was not amused.

"Yakutsk? Do you have any idea how far away that is? I'm not spending four days on the train for a few roubles."

"There's such a thing as a plane, you know." Anton retorted. "Besides, we're not just talking about a few roubles. I convinced my uncle to invest in 500 units. Spring break is coming up next week. The new miners will be shipped directly to Yakutsk, and we can take these units with us in our luggage. We'll cover the cost of your plane ticket, accommodation, and all the vodka you can drink. What do you think?" Yuri didn't have any other plans, and he really enjoyed working with the miners. Dmitry agreed just to go along for the ride.

Arriving in Yakutsk, they were surprised to see snow still on the ground. Anton's uncle Josef met them at the airport. On the way to their hotel, he told them it was one of the coldest cities in Russia. They dropped off their bags at his flat and went directly to the dam. As they drove along the river road to the dam, Josef also told them about its history. It had originally been built to power the mining and smelting industry in Soviet times, but the fall of the Soviet Union and increasing competition on the world market had ended any hope of the city becoming an industrial centre.

Josef was quite concerned. The dam was fully operational, but since it was not generating enough revenue, it was poorly maintained. He was afraid that it could fail and endanger the towns and villages downstream.

Soon they arrived and met the director of the dam, an old friend of Josef's. He gave them a tour of the facility, including the turbines. He said that of the 650 megawatt capacity of the damn, it produced an average of 450 megawatts per year. Of that, only about 100 megawatts were used by nearby mines, and another 50 megawatts supplied the surrounding residences and businesses – overall, an average of 70 per cent of the energy produced by the dam went unused.

Over tea and sweets in his office, the director asked them about their plans and the requirement for the facility. Yuri told him about the power requirements of the mining units, and they discussed the cost of the infrastructure involved. Dmitry attempted to tell the director about how Bitcoin could free the world from financial slavery, but the director was evidently more concerned about the bottom line. When Anton described the Bitcoin market and how much he'd made from mining in the past year, the director took more notice.

When the Bitcoin discussion trailed off, they put on their coats and went out for a walk around the surrounding area. They mapped out the sector near the dam and determined that an old warehouse would be an optimal location. It would need upgrading to accommodate the transformers and cables. The director agreed to cover the cost of the installation on the condition that it would be covered by their first mining profits. They would start building that summer once the upgrades were complete.

Yuri and Dmitry would return in summer – they'd been looking for summer jobs anyway, and it was really the best time to visit Siberia. Back in Moscow, they finished out the semester and finally returning to Yakutsk after their exams. They arrived to find the warehouse wired up and ready to go.

Their first task – getting all the mining units up and running – came with several challenges: making sure the power was balanced, spacing the units evenly so they wouldn't overheat, and designing the network to avoid single points of failure and minimise downtime when upgrades or repairs were needed. Optimising the software on each machine, Yuri felt as if he was working on an assembly line. It was exhausting, but the two of them were learning a lot.

One day, Dmitry went to town to buy some groceries. When he returned, Yuri noticed there was something different about him. He seemed euphoric.

"I want to become a farmer!" he said, falling back onto his cot. Yuri was shocked.

"Have you lost your mind? What about engineering?"

"You don't understand," he said, "I just met a girl in town, and I asked her about her work. She's a farmer and very passionate about it. I tried to get her to come here to see what we're doing, but as she's not interested in Bitcoin at all, I told her that we're starting an agricultural project and that we need her to come here as a consultant to help us set it up." Yuri looked at him, incredulous.

"There's just one problem with your plan, genius. We don't have a farm."

"Listen, I've got an idea. We can build a greenhouse structure on top of the warehouse and use all of the heat from the miners to warm it. If we set up the greenhouse with hydroponics, it won't be too heavy, and we can find some scrap steel to reinforce the structure. If we route water from the reservoir, we can use gravity to pump the water through the system. And Anton told me about an abandoned airbase near here where we can salvage materials."

Yuri shook his head. "No, you've really lost it this time. All of this work for a girl? Go ahead if you want, but count me out." Yuri turned back to his laptop.

"She's got a sister," Dmitry added slyly. Yuri thought about it for a moment and then replied.

"How big of a greenhouse are we talking about?"

They went to Anton's uncle and told him about the idea. He was very supportive. He said they always faced shortages of fresh produce during the long winters, but in the past, heating a greenhouse wasn't cost effective.

At the weekend, they borrowed a truck from Anton's uncle and drove to the airbase. A pair of very bored soldiers stood guard at the gate and waved them through. They arrived at a hangar, unloaded some tools, and set about breaking it down.

Yuri was hesitant. "Are you sure we have permission to do this?"

Anton's uncle reassured him, "I went to school with the colonel in charge here. I gave him a bottle of vodka and some beluga caviar. We're all clear."

After the truck was half-filled with girders, they drove over to a rusted water tank with lengths of pipe running to it and began dismantling that as well.

Back at the warehouse, Dmitry drew up a schematic for the greenhouse, but they still had work to do setting up and optimising the miners. So, as a temporary measure, they left the materials for the greenhouse in a great heap nearby.

Once they got all the miners online, they dedicated more time to the greenhouse. They enlisted the help of a welder to reinforce key points of the structure and installed walkways along the roof. They cut a hole in the roof to serve as an entrance and put a ladder up to the hole. On the roof, they bowed lengths of plastic piping into semi-circles to form a framework, over which they laid plastic sheeting to cover the greenhouse itself. Yelena and her sister Katy were invited as expert consultants, advising on the optimum layout. Dmitry and Yuri suddenly became intensely interested in plant nutrient balances and ideal pH levels for strawberries.

They spent the rest of the summer tending to the greenhouse, teaching some of the dam workers how to maintain the miners, exploring the countryside with Yelena and Katy, catching fish in forest lakes, and generally enjoying life. When the time came to return to Moscow, they left with reluctance.

Anton's uncle and his colleagues did their best to keep the mine running smoothly. He got the greenhouse functional and producing strawberries by fall, but a number of technical problems appeared with the miners. Despite the harsh Siberian winter, the greenhouse was still too hot.

Yuri spent hours on the phone trying to walk through the technical issues and get all the miners back online, with no success. Finally, they agreed to return during the winter holiday.

Yuri ordered the replacement parts they needed before they left and had everything with him when they arrived, so getting all the miners back online didn't take long. Dmitry considered installing extra vents in the greenhouse but decided against it after calculating it would be a waste.

While in town visiting Yelena, he noticed the municipal swimming pool was closed. She told him they shut it every winter because of the cold. He immediately proposed that they route the heat from the miners into the town, which turned out to be quite a feat of engineering. First, he had to calculate the total heat load produced by the miners and the volume of the greenhouse. Then he calculated the amount of heat needed to maintain a steady temperature inside the greenhouse and the percentage they would need to capture.

Next, with the help of the townsfolk, who had already been enjoying the winter strawberries, they fashioned shrouds that routed the heat to a water tank and laid insulated pipes to the swimming pool. The heat was sufficient to warm the water to around 70° Celsius, which was then pumped to the pool and elevated the temperature to a comfortable 28° via a heat exchanger.

The cooled water returned to the miner warehouse, where it was heated again in a closed loop.

By this time, Yuri and Dmitry were becoming quite popular in the village. Under the expert management of Anton's uncle, the greenhouse was producing fresh strawberries through the winter and generating supplemental income. With the cheap electricity, the Bitcoin profits were substantial, and Anton's uncle and the director offered them jobs maintaining and expanding the facility.

With a bit of encouragement from Yelena and Katy, it wasn't hard to convince them to accept. And so it came to pass that on clear winter days, you could catch Yuri and Dmitry sunbathing in Siberian strawberry fields.

✳ ✳ ✳

Is Bitcoin Killing the Planet?

Satoshi Nakamoto may have found a solution to a longstanding computing problem, but Bitcoin's energy consumption has attracted its fair share of criticism. You may have seen headlines like "Bitcoin mining consumes more electricity than Switzerland and Chile combined" or "Bitcoin is killing the earth".

While the amount of energy consumed by the Bitcoin network is astonishing, it's an absolute exaggeration to point to it as destructive to the environment. When Satoshi Nakamoto designed Bitcoin, he understood that energy consumption could eventually grow very high.

"Bitcoin generation should end up where it's cheapest. Maybe that will be in cold climates where there's electric heat, where it would be essentially free."

There are indeed many possibilities for recycling heat, and a number of these techniques have already been implemented by Bitcoin miners. The story of Yuri and his friends details a few of these methods, but there are also many other industrial uses for waste heat. And due to the competitive nature of the Bitcoin mining market, most of the energy used by the Bitcoin network is unused renewable energy that would otherwise go to waste.

So far, the majority of Bitcoin mining has gravitated toward hydroelectric energy. In many locations, hydroelectric power is cheap, and the supply exceeds the demand for much of the year. A recent study found that Bitcoin mining powered by renewable energy makes up approximately 74 per cent of Bitcoin mining worldwide.

So it can hardly be argued that Bitcoin is contributing significantly to carbon emissions any more than other industries. Furthermore, as the cryptocurrency industry grows, Bitcoin is generating value and creating jobs. Taking this into account, it's difficult to say that the carbon emissions generated by Bitcoin are really a waste.

The accusations levelled against Bitcoin are not only baseless – in fact, the opposite is true; Bitcoin has the potential to support the growth of renewable energy and actually help the environment.

Demand Response and Energy Efficiency

Much of the world is operating on antiquated and highly inefficient electrical grids. The inefficiency of the world's energy grids makes electricity more expensive for ordinary people – it also makes it more expensive to develop renewable energy sources.

For example, consider the concept of *capacity factor*. Capacity factor is used in the energy industry to describe the ratio of the total possible output of a power plant to its actual output. For example, if a solar farm is capable of producing 1,200 kilowatt-hours per day, and only 800 kilowatt-hours are used on a given day, then the capacity factor of that solar farm is two-thirds, or 66 per cent, for that day. The following chart illustrates the approximate capacity factor for different kinds of energy during a two-year period.

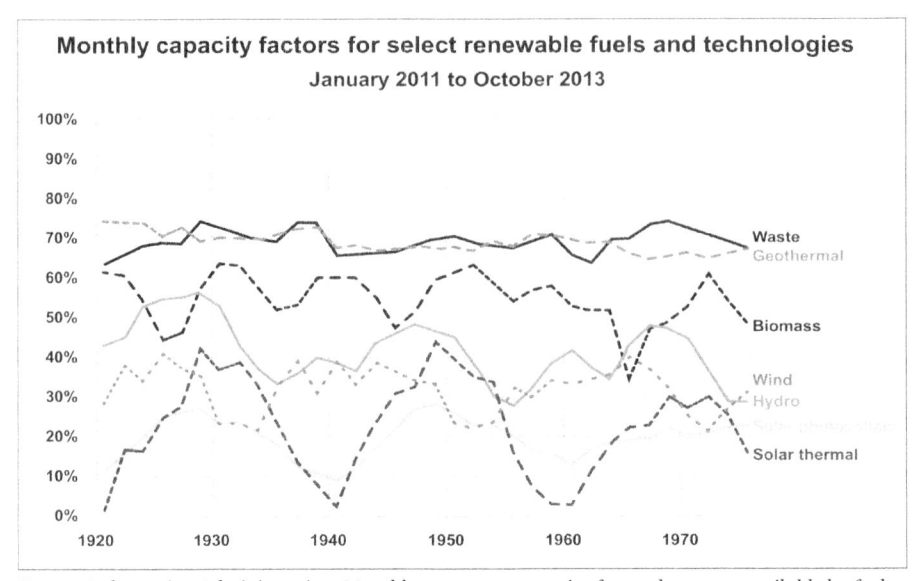

Monthly capacity factors for select renewable fuels and technologies
January 2011 to October 2013

(Chart showing capacity factors from 0% to 100% on y-axis, years 1920 to 1970 on x-axis, with lines for Waste, Geothermal, Biomass, Wind, Hydro, and Solar thermal)

Energy Information Administration. Monthly generator capacity factor data now available by fuel and technology. 15 January 2014.

Renewable energy sources like wind and solar are currently less profitable than other forms of power generation because of their low capacity factors. So why do renewable energy sources like wind and solar have such low capacity factors? Other forms of energy can be scaled up and down according to demand. By contrast, the amount of energy produced by solar and wind depends on the elements, so when energy is abundant, there is not always an abundance of demand. This means investors who build wind or solar energy plants cannot always find buyers for the energy they produce.

Anyone who has ever looked at installing solar panels can tell you that one of the most expensive aspects of solar is storing the energy. Even if energy is sold back to the grid, it often involves installing specialised equipment, and even then, there are regional fluctuations in demand. A certain amount of electricity is also lost as leakage when transported over long distances.

Even with conventional methods of power generation like coal, energy is lost when furnaces have to heat up or cool down to accommodate seasonal variations in demand. The more power producers are able to predict demand, the better they optimise efficiency.

Bitcoin has the unique property of generating demand for electricity anywhere, at any time. Bitcoin mining has a very light footprint in terms of the space needed, so it can be installed on location at power plants, standing by and ready to consume every excess kilowatt of power produced. This effectively acts as a guarantee that energy producers will have guaranteed buyers for 100 per cent of the electricity they produce.

While some people may not see the value in Bitcoin, a great many people, like the characters in this book, do see great value in it. As such, it has economic value, and as long as it does, there will be a direct method of converting electricity to money. As cryptocurrency mining becomes increasingly integrated with energy infrastructure, higher efficiency will translate to better profit margins for power producers. These savings will be passed on to consumers in the form of lower rates, and it will also shift the profitability calculations for renewable energy in particular.

This can have a major positive impact on the market for renewable energy technology worldwide.

Driving the Market for Renewable Energy

As concerned as we may be about the environment, the fact is that most of us are unwilling to pay double or triple the electric bill for the sake of cleaner energy. We can dislike coal-burning power plants all we want – ultimately, it's economic concerns that shape the character of the energy market.

Bitcoin is unique as a truly mobile industry. Other industries depend on other considerations for their profitability – for example, access to ports, markets, and certain raw materials. Since Bitcoin is a purely digital good and can be transported anywhere, almost instantaneously, miners can travel to wherever the energy is cheapest. It's already common to hear of miners relocating thousands of miles away to access cheap hydroelectric energy.

For example, many cryptocurrency miners have relocated to Iceland, where they take advantage of abundant geothermal energy sources. Geothermal vents in Iceland have long been recognised as a cheap and clean energy source, but until now, no industry was able to really take advantage of them. The same applies to many remote areas that are abundant in solar or wind energy.

One of the major costs of starting a solar farm is the land. Normally, the main market for energy is in residential, industrial, or commercial areas, and property tends to be more expensive in these areas. This leaves investors with the choice of either paying for expensive land or paying for expensive transmission lines to deliver the energy to market.

With Bitcoin mining, solar panels can be installed in remote areas where land is inexpensive and where very little additional infrastructure is needed. This means many renewable energy installations that would never have been profitable in the past can now become viable.

This applies not only to commercial energy production ventures but also to small-scale producers. Consider the thought process a homeowner weighing up whether or not to install solar panels on the roof. One of the most expensive components of a solar system is energy storage. Battery systems are also much more prone to failure than photovoltaic cells themselves. If you decide to install solar panels without a storage system, it's much cheaper, but you'll end up producing far more energy than you can ever use.

Of course, you could always run the washing machine or other appliances on solar during sunlight hours and capture some savings in this way. But in the final analysis, it's probably still much cheaper just to purchase energy from the grid. If you can turn 100 per cent of the energy produced by your solar panels directly into cash, however, this could very easily tip the balance in favour of a solar system.

This same logic applies in a variety of situations. Consider, for example, remote homes, businesses, or communities trying to decide whether to install the lines to connect to the grid or use wind, water, solar, or geothermal energy. The possibility to convert energy into cash anywhere, anytime has tremendous economic implications.

This means that Bitcoin and other proof-of-work currencies could drive a huge increase in demand for renewable energy technologies. As demand for any technology grows, the research and development that goes into that technology also grow, and research and development lower the overall cost of the technology. As the cost of the technology decreases, the number of profitable applications of the technology increases, leading to a virtuous cycle of renewable energy adoption.

The impact of Bitcoin mining is not small. At the time of writing, it's estimated that as much as one per cent of the world's electricity is used for Bitcoin mining, and the network continues to grow. So really, we should all be very excited about the possibility of Bitcoin accelerating the shift towards cleaner energy and more efficient economies.

But several projects have attempted to develop alternatives to proof-of-work-based consensus. Some of these alternative consensus systems have been justified by the criticism of Bitcoin's high energy consumption. Will these alternative consensus mechanisms be able to dethrone Bitcoin?

Is Bitcoin Going to Zero?

Obviously, this entire book is based on the premise that Bitcoin and cryptocurrency are going to change the world. Some sceptics are surely wondering, "What if it all fails?" Since there are so many interests involved in money, there are plenty of incentives to spread doubt about different currencies. Some of the most common narratives include the possibility that quantum computing could render obsolete the encryption algorithms which make cryptocurrency possible. Another is that governments could all somehow band together to ban cryptocurrency.

Quantum computing currently can't perform the type of

operations necessary to crack the algorithms that secure most cryptocurrencies, and even if at some point they can, research into quantum resistance is also underway. Moreover, it's unlikely that *all* governments will ban cryptocurrencies, especially now that they realise they can tax it and profit.

A more realistic possibility is that other cryptocurrencies could eclipse Bitcoin in the same way that Facebook took over market share from MySpace. This is also unlikely, however, because cryptocurrencies do not compete solely based on technology – they also compete based on ideology. Because cryptocurrency is so political, the design of each currency is deeply affected by moral values and beliefs and, as such, appeals to those who hold those beliefs. The values of the cypherpunk community are hardcoded into the Bitcoin protocol.

These values resonate strongly with libertarians and followers of the Austrian school of economics as well. Ethereum, on the other hand, is sometimes described as Keynesian in its approach. The ideology, in turn, affects the technical choices that are made. For example, Bitcoin, as a counter to the fiat currency system, has a fixed supply. Other currencies try to pursue more price stability and transaction speed in order to be used for day-to-day purchase. Generally speaking, having a more stable exchange rate requires more centralised control, which many reject on ideological grounds.

All of these debates and discussions are vastly complicated by how much money is involved. The cryptocurrency industry is now worth hundreds of billions and will likely soon reach into the trillions, and much of this valuation is based on ideas. The more people you can convince of the value of your ideas (or the ideas behind the cryptocurrency that you own), the more likely they are to invest in it and drive up its value. It's always hard to tell if the people promoting an idea sincerely believe it is the best thing for the network or if they are only promoting it to increase the value of their own investment portfolio. There's also no shortage of unscrupulous individuals willing to lie and deceive to turn a quick profit.

Many investors stay with Bitcoin simply because there is no doubt about Satoshi Nakamoto's sincerity. Since cryptocurrency had no economic value when Bitcoin was invented, there is much more trust that Satoshi was not trying to scam anyone. This has not been the case with the many currencies created since Bitcoin.

However, any currency that can get people to believe in it, whether for ideological or monetary reasons or both, can maintain a monetary value. Bitcoin clearly has the biggest following, and since the usefulness of a currency depends on how many people are willing to accept it, value may well continue to converge on Bitcoin, making it the true gold standard of the cryptocurrency ecosystem.

Another factor that points to Bitcoin's long-term survival is the wealth of Bitcoin proponents. As Bitcoin's value grows, the early adopters become wealthier, and with this wealth comes more economic and political power. These early adopters are likely to use their wealth and influence to protect the interests of Bitcoin since the value of their wealth will depend on it. They may do this by sponsoring research and development into technologies like quantum-resistant cryptography or lobbying for supportive legislation.

The most exciting part of this is that it is not at all too late to be an early adopter. By most estimates, less than 1.5% of the world's population has ever bought or used Bitcoin.

5. Farhan Kazdi

Escaping the Police State

Farhan grew up on a farm not far from Tehran. His father, Ali, grew saffron, and his grandfather before him had done the same, so everyone always assumed that Farhan would follow in his father's footsteps. As a boy, though, Farhan developed other interests. He would lie in the fields filled with purple saffron flowers and see military planes flying overhead. He also overheard anxious discussions about the possibility of war. He would ask his father why there might be a war, and Ali told him as much as he could. Farhan developed a deep interest in politics.

He studied hard in school and was always eager to learn more about the world, so it was no surprise when he was awarded a scholarship to university. Ali was sceptical of the government scholarship but wanted to see his son happy and encouraged him nonetheless.

Ali had been just a young child during the Iranian revolution, but he had seen many of his relatives who had supported it turn into fanatics. He was saddened but not surprised when his son came home from university after his first year thinking and talking the same way. Unlike most Iranians, Ali didn't like to talk about politics -- in his opinion, it brought few benefits and seemed to cause plenty of trouble. So whenever Farhan tried to bring up politics on his visits home, Ali remained silent or changed the subject.

Farhan was frustrated by what he saw as his father's apathy. He truly believed that his nation was standing up against the bullying of America and Israel and saw it as a David and Goliath struggle against tyranny. How could his father not be proud of the nation demanding justice against the oppressors of the world?

Farhan also accepted that some economic sacrifices were necessary for this struggle, but his father complained of the crippling sanctions and his inability to get a good price for the farm's produce. Farhan argued that it was a necessary hardship to promote the interests of the nation. Nonetheless, it hurt him to see his father's farm suffering. At times, he had to wonder why his father had to suffer because of politics that he had nothing to do with.

Farhan graduated with a degree in communications, and just before graduation, he was offered a job at IRIB, Islamic Republic of Iran Broadcasting, where he had worked as an intern in his final year of university. Although Ali disagreed with the path Farhan had chosen, he was still proud of his son.

Farhan dived enthusiastically into his work. He started out reporting on local crime news but soon rose up the editorial ladder, covering major economic and political stories. He so genuinely believed in the goodness of his country that he never thought of what he was doing as propaganda – he sincerely believed he was helping inform the Iranian people about important events in the world.

He reported on Iran's home-grown automobile and arms industry, showcased breakthroughs in the nuclear program, and lavished praise on Iranian scientists. He wrote editorial pieces lampooning the hypocrisy of Western politicians. He also developed human interest pieces, highlighting the struggles of the Iranian people in the face of ongoing sanctions and economic hardship.

One of the stories he covered was on Bitcoin, and in particular illegal Bitcoin mining in mosques. Since mosques received free electricity provided by the state, some clever individuals had decided to take advantage by mining Bitcoin. At first, he was critical of what he saw as opportunistic behaviour by the miners, but as he learned more about Bitcoin, he saw in it a solution to several problems. Since it was possible to send Bitcoin to anyone with an internet connection, he realised that his father could sell the family farm's produce overseas.

He spoke with his father about it, and Ali was immediately interested. Perhaps his son's chosen career was not all bad if it enabled him to learn about things that helped the family. Farhan's brother, Reza, set about advertising their saffron online and within a few months had secured several customers. Farhan spoke with the director of the office about the possibility of creating a feature on the use of Bitcoin by entrepreneurs to circumvent sanctions. The director agreed, and the piece generated quite a buzz.

At the end of his third year at IRIB, he received an award for his outstanding contributions. But what appeared to be a brilliant career in the making took an unexpected turn when, one day, the director of Farhan's office handed him an assignment about Iran's missile program.

At first glance, it looked like a routine story – the Iranian military was testing a new missile with an unprecedented range and payload. Farhan was to prepare a piece about its capabilities and strategic impact.

He travelled to the research headquarters the next day to interview the head of the program. Everything went smoothly, but as he was leaving, he noticed a sleek, silver Bentley pulling out of the parking lot of the building. This in itself would have been remarkable, as such cars were quite rare in a country where much of the population lived on no more than a few dollars a day, but Farhan had seen this car before on multiple occasions at the Iranian Consultative Assembly.

His curiosity was piqued, but he was so busy with his work that he didn't pay it any mind. He dug into the documentation on the development of the new missile, its technical specifications, and the project's budget. Looking deeply at the budget, however, he noticed some irregularities. The missile radar altimeters, an essential part of the navigation system, were priced considerably higher than those he had seen when he'd worked on a similar project during his internship. The company that had manufactured the altimeters was not listed, so he called several manufacturers in the Tehran area to ask about them.

Only one company manufactured components that met the description exactly – Isfahan Industries. He called the office and explained to the company representative that he was researching a piece on the new missile program and wanted more info on the components and their cost of manufacture. The representative was happy to oblige and told him he would send over some documentation on their production process.

The next day, when Farhan came to work, there was an excited air in the office. A standoff was happening over an American ship that had been seized after entering Iranian territorial waters. The Americans were demanding the immediate return of the ship and threatening retaliatory strikes if their demands were not met.

Farhan had to drop everything and head to the Consultative Assembly, where an emergency session was underway. The politicians were debating which course of action to take – returning the ship and bowing to the American demands would make them look weak, some argued. Others pointed out that there was little or no strategic value in keeping the ship and that the temporary seizure was punishment enough.

Then the head of the judiciary, Hasan Shirazi, gave a rousing speech. He spoke in highly emotional terms, citing the suffering of the innocent Iranian children under the ongoing sanctions, how children were getting sick and dying from lack of medicine. Shirazi insisted that force was the only language that America understood. Farhan eagerly took notes on the speech and was filled with outrage by Shirazi's emotive words.

As the session ended and he waited outside with other journalists for a statement from the president, he saw Shirazi exit the assembly building with an armed escort. The same silver Bentley he'd seen before, driven by a chauffeur, appeared. Shirazi entered the car and it sped off.

Two things bothered Farhan. First, if Shirazi was so concerned about the welfare of Iranian children, why was he driving around in a British car that cost more than most Iranians would make in their lifetime? And second, what was the head of the judiciary doing at a weapons research and development centre?

The car was so unique he was sure it must be the same one he'd seen the previous day, but he found it somehow odd that the head of the judiciary would visit a weapons plant. Farhan began to investigate Shirazi's background. He had actively opposed all negotiations with the American government and had consistently pushed to increase defence spending. He was regarded as strictly religious, kept a beard and wore traditional Iranian garb and a turban, but Farhan was surprised to find that Shirazi's son, Ashkan, spent most of his time in France, where Western tabloids frequently featured photographs of him escorting French or Italian supermodels in and out of his Champs-Élysées townhouse.

Farhan was fascinated but a bit angry. He had heard Shirazi denouncing the moral corruption of the West on a number of occasions, yet his own son seemed to be living a life of luxury in France. He wanted to know how Ashkan was paying for this lifestyle. When he looked into Ashkan's professional background, he was surprised to see that Ashkan was on the board of Isfahan Industries.

Later that day, the pamphlet from Isfahan Industries appeared, and Farhan found that the altimeter components cost less than a third of the price quoted in the missile development budget.

Farhan didn't want to jump to conclusions, so he scheduled an appointment with the director in charge of the program. Perhaps there was an explanation for all this, he thought.

When he arrived at the director's office later that week, he began to explain to him his concerns. The director's face paled. He looked at Farhan very seriously and said, "Look, for your own good, I'm going to give you some advice. Drop this investigation. Forget about it."

"What, why? If there is corruption, the anti-corruption committee needs to know about it, and if there is wrongdoing, those involved need to be brought to account," Farhan replied angrily.

"I'm begging you, don't make trouble for me. I have a family to feed. I don't have any choice in this matter. If I don't do what I'm told, he'll destroy me. And he'll destroy you too if you don't stop."

"Who?" Farhan asked.

"I thought you'd figured that out by now. Let's just say there's no point in going to the anti-corruption committee. Look, you seem very nice, so just forget any of this ever happened and move on with your life."

Farhan was shocked. He realised that as head of the judiciary, Shirazi was also the supervisor of the anti-corruption committee. Stunned, he thanked the director and left the office.

On the way back to his office, resolve slowly formed in him. He had to take a stand against this. When he realised that Shirazi might be pushing for war for the sake of personal profit, he felt nauseous. He knew that if he didn't do anything, he'd never be able to live with himself.

Back at the office, he went directly to his boss and suggested they run an exposé. At first, his boss was incredulous, but as Farhan showed him the evidence he had collected, he was shocked. He gave him the go-ahead to start working on it.

Farhan began working day and night gathering data. The deeper he dug, the more dirt he found. Shirazi had more than 50 bank accounts where large sums of government funds were held, presumably to collect interest. Farhan found multiple corruption investigations into businesses linked to Shirazi that had been inexplicably dismissed. He also saw a number of competitors to Shirazi's businesses who had been convicted on weak evidence on charges ranging from corruption to espionage. In some cases, Shirazi's competitors had been handed the death penalty.

Farhan became absorbed by his research. He stayed up late into the night working, and his co-workers even had to remind him to eat. Then, suddenly, his boss appeared.

"Farhan, sorry, we're cancelling that piece on Shirazi."

"What?" After all the work he had put in, Farhan was devastated.

"I know you did a lot of work on this, but it's not up to me. This order comes from the top. Just forget about it. It's just a misunderstanding."

Farhan understood what was happening. He gathered all of his notes and documents into a portfolio, went to a nearby copy shop and began scanning everything and loading it to a USB drive. He wasn't going to be silenced. If he couldn't publish it in the newspaper, he'd start a blog.

Just then, his brother called him. He was in town buying some irrigation supplies and invited Farhan to lunch. Farhan was relieved because he really felt the need to talk to someone. When he met his brother, everything poured out. Reza was very worried but sympathetic. He advised Farhan.

"I know you're upset, but don't do anything hasty. I don't want you to get into trouble."

"But I can't just do nothing! It's like there's a fire lit inside of me, and I have to put it out." Farhan replied.

"Isn't there some way that you can release this information without Shirazi knowing that it's you?"

Farhan thought about it, but he didn't know how he could publish his work without revealing his identity. But Reza had always been tech savvy, and he offered to help him anonymise himself. Reza gave him some tips about methods he could use.

When Farhan got home, he started researching the encryption techniques Reza had told him about, but he quickly ran into a major problem. Most of the websites where he could download the software he needed to anonymise himself were blocked by the government firewall.

In the past, he had always assumed that censorship was necessary to prevent the spread of Western corruption and immorality. Now he began to wonder if it was not about stopping people like him from getting the truth out. He phoned Reza to ask him for help.

Reza had learned all about evading government censorship when downloading banned music videos as a teenager, so he walked Farhan through the process of circumventing the controls.

Once Farhan broke through the censorship wall, it was as if a new world opened to him. He found the blogs of multiple Iranian journalists in exile, detailing all manner of abuses he had never imagined. He pored over page after page of documents as if in a trance.

Then he began to work, compiling documents, cross-referencing old articles on Shirazi and his businesses, drawing tables and charts to demonstrate inconsistencies, and editing video clips of interviews. He was ready to start publishing his findings, but he knew that if his work was traced back to him, Shirazi would find him.

All of the web-hosting services in Iran were regulated by the interior ministry, and Farhan had learned in his research that Shirazi's daughter was married to the interior minister. He called Reza again, who agreed to do some research on the topic for him. Reza called back a few hours later and told him he'd discovered a web hosting service in Sweden that accepted Bitcoin as a method of payment.

Ali had heard about Farhan's work from Reza and was very happy that his son was taking a more sceptical view of the government. He agreed to donate some of the farm's Bitcoin profits to Farhan so he could begin hosting his blog.

In the weeks that this was all happening, Farhan's performance at the office was declining. He began to lose focus – the stories he was covering seemed so meaningless compared to what he was working on at home. The final straw came when his boss asked him to do a retrospective on Shirazi's career.

The assignment required him to highlight Shirazi's humble village background and how he'd risen as a hero of the revolution. It was to include clips of Shirazi sitting with farmers, opening orphanages, and dealing out hard justice to violent criminals and spies. As Farhan read the description, he felt rage swelling up inside him.

He got up from his desk, left the office, walked to a park and sat on a bench. He was in a daze. A teenager approached him and tried to sell him a newspaper. Farhan's face went pale – on the front page was a headline announcing Shirazi's bid for the presidency.

He phoned his boss and told him he was ill and wouldn't be coming to work. He drafted his resignation letter and submitted it that day.

As he continued his work at home, his contacts with the community of Iranian journalists in exile became more extensive. They shared troves of documents with him, and he followed a trail of corruption, leading to a network of officials at every level of government.

He became so obsessed with his work that he didn't notice the days go by. He began publishing his findings and built up a following of Iranian dissidents, both inside and outside the country. One day his brother came to visit him. When Reza saw Farhan, he was appalled.

"You're as thin as a stick! You haven't been eating well, have you?"

"I've got some flatbread here." Farhan snapped defensively, pointing to some bread he'd been eating. Reza looked sceptically at the plastic bag of dried bread on Farhan's desk. Just then, there was a knock on the door. Farhan opened it, and Reza overheard a heated conversation with the owner of the apartment. Farhan hastily promised to pay next week.

"Next week? That's what you said last week! Look, if you can't get it together, you need to get out."

Farhan timidly promised to find a solution and closed the door.

"You're not doing too well, are you, brother? What happened to your job?" Reza asked.

Farhan told him about what he'd been learning and about the report his boss had asked him to do on Shirazi. As usual, Reza was full of bright ideas. He suggested starting a crowdfunding campaign.

Reza helped him create a Bitcoin wallet and get the campaign started. Farhan's network of colleagues in exile and followers supported him and helped spread the word. The donations poured in from countries as diverse as New Zealand, Kenya, Canada, and Brazil. Within a week, he'd gathered enough funding to cover his expenses for another six months.

Each blog post and video he created revealed more evidence of Shirazi's hypocrisy. The problem was reaching the audience inside Iran. Social media were banned, and the domestic alternatives were tightly controlled, but his followers began distributing the videos through instant messaging services.

One day, an anonymous hacker contacted Farhan and offered to help him access Shirazi's bank records. Farhan happily accepted. When he received the records and went over them, he was able to draw a map of Shirazi's entire network.

Preparing the post was a huge amount of work. He had to research the background of over 75 different government officials and businessmen, make the connections between their dealings and Shirazi, and all of this without arousing suspicion. There was no doubt in Farhan's mind – this was the most damning evidence he'd collected on Shirazi's network so far. But when he went to publish it, he found that his blog was no longer online.

Puzzled, he tried contacting the web hosting company via email but received no reply. He did a web search for the company, and a news article appeared at the top of the search. There had been a break-in at the company's data centre, and one security guard had been hospitalised. The intruder had accessed the servers and disappeared.

Farhan felt his pulse quicken. He knew when he had started that something like this might happen, and he was prepared to face the consequences. He knew that Shirazi had connections in the Revolutionary Guards Corps and that they had a network of operatives around the world. If they had gained access to the server, they could have deleted his blog. He realised that he now risked losing all of his work from the past months. The only remaining copy of the data was on his laptop.

He immediately called Reza and told him what had happened. Reza seemed worried.

"If they got access to the server logs, they may be able to use the data to find you," he told Farhan. "Maybe you should get out of there."

"Before I do anything, I have to make sure my research gets backed up. If anyone gets a hold of my laptop, all my work will be lost."

"Well, if the files aren't too big, you could try backing it up on a decentralised network," Reza suggested.

"A what?" Farhan had heard the word before in the context of his reporting on Bitcoin, but he didn't know how it could help him secure his work.

"It's just a secure, distributed form of data storage. Use some of the Bitcoin you got from the crowdfund, and buy some coins from a platform. Then compress all your data and upload it –." Farhan heard a loud noise and voices in the background. "I have to go," Reza said, and the line abruptly went silent.

Farhan was worried. Could they have used the data in the server to trace the blog back to Reza? It was Reza who had helped him create the blog.

Farhan began researching the distributed blockchains Reza had told him about. He discovered a platform that had been used by Vietnamese journalists to secure their data and purchased some of the network's tokens on a cryptocurrency exchange. He compressed his work as Reza had told him and used the tokens to pay a web portal to upload the data. The videos were too large to upload, so he was only able to save the documents.

He was about to forward a link to the data to his colleagues when he heard footsteps in the hallway outside his apartment. Moments later, the door crashed open, and eight uniformed men carrying AK-47s stormed into the room.

They seized him, handcuffed him, and forced him to sit on the floor in the corner. He watched as they tore his furniture apart, cut open his mattress, threw his books on the floor, and collected all of his documents into cardboard boxes. After a time, two of the men dragged him out and threw him into the back of a truck that was waiting in the street.

He was blindfolded, so he didn't know where they were taking him, but he soon found himself being interrogated in a dark room. Most of the questions were about his files and the server in Sweden. He was careful not to tell them about the copy of the files on the blockchain. Once the interrogator was satisfied that the only copies of the data were on his laptop and the server in Sweden, Farhan was taken to solitary confinement.

After several months in the dank cell, an officer came to him and told him that he'd made bail, adding that he was to stay away from journalism and find a new career. If he didn't, the officer warned him, there would be consequences.

Farhan, pale and ragged, was escorted to the building's reception, where he was met by his father and brother. After an emotional embrace, they drove back to the farm. Farhan was happy to see his mother. He had often wondered in the prison if he'd ever see her again. Farhan spent the night in his old room and had his first good night's sleep in months.

In the morning, over breakfast, he discussed the situation with Ali and Reza. They had used the deed to the farm as security for his release, but charges were still pending against him in court. He was accused of working as an agent for an American news agency and spreading false rumours to defame the character of Iranian officials.

Reza asked him if he had managed to save the documents. Farhan replied that he had. But they all understood that if he published his research, he would probably never see the light of day again.

There was a long silence, and Ali stared intently at the table, deep in thought. Finally, he spoke.

"Farhan, you have to leave the country and publish everything."

"But father, you'll lose the farm! This is all we have," Farhan replied.

"All the wealth in the world won't do us any good if we have the power to do something against this evil, and we stand by in silence. We would share in the crimes that you've worked so hard to uncover. Don't worry, son. We are strong enough to carry the burden of doing what is right."

"We talked about this while you were in prison. I've been in contact with a smuggler in Tabriz who can get you over the Turkish border. You can go to Istanbul and stay with your cousin Hussein. He'll help you figure out your next step."

It was a difficult decision. Farhan didn't know if he'd ever see his family again. But he knew he'd never be able to live with himself if he backed down.

After a tearful goodbye, he boarded a bus to Tabriz. His phone had been confiscated by the police, but Reza had given him his. When he arrived, he spent the night in a hotel. The smuggler came to meet him in the morning. He paid the smuggler's fee, which took almost all his father's savings.

By the time they reached the border, it was dark. The smuggler shut off the headlights and parked in a stand of trees. They waited in silence as a border patrol passed by. When its red taillights disappeared behind a hill, they sped across towards the nearest town.

Waiting for the bus to Istanbul, Farhan bought a Turkish SIM card, loaded it with internet credit, and navigated to a browser interface for the blockchain where he'd saved the files. He found them and downloaded them. He then joined a group chat he'd created earlier with a number of his journalist contacts and sent the file with a link to the undeletable copy.

The report circulated like wildfire. It exposed not only Shirazi's crimes but his entire network of accomplices, with detailed accounts of how much they had pilfered from the Iranian people. Angry mobs stormed the Ministry of Justice in Tehran, and the soldiers were ordered to fire on the protestors. But the report had reached the soldiers as well by that time, and resentful of their low salaries in comparison to the wealth Shirazi had been raking in, they refused to fire.

Shirazi was forced to flee on foot and narrowly escaped with his life. The leaders of the protest established a citizens' tribunal, and those implicated in the scandal were stripped of their assets in Iran. But most of their wealth had been safeguarded in bank accounts in offshore tax havens. And so they were imprisoned, to be released on the condition they return their stolen wealth. One by one, they made the necessary phone calls and had the funds released.

As it happened, with Shirazi and his accomplices gone, many of the pro-war voices in the consultative assembly disappeared, and negotiations with America started again. Farhan was cleared of wrongdoing, and after just two short years in exile, he returned home to a hero's welcome.

As the country opened up to the world, the economy began to improve. Ferraris or Lamborghinis no longer cruised the streets of Tehran; instead, family-owned businesses and co-working spaces began to appear. The IRIB dissolved, and Farhan's boss called him up, asking him to head the investigative division of a new private news agency.

The work of protecting society from corruption was far from over. But with free money powering free information, life had become much more difficult for those who seek power through lies and deception.

* * *

Absolute Power Corrupts Absolutely

According to the Human Rights Foundation, more than 50 per cent of the world's population lives under authoritarian regimes, but the problems associated with authoritarianism should concern us all. History has shown how quickly a democratic country can descend into totalitarianism. While centralisation of power is sometimes politically expedient or even necessary, any time there is a concentration of power, there is also the risk of it falling into the wrong hands.

The increasing pervasiveness of surveillance represents just such a concentration of power. One of the revelations of the Edward Snowden leaks was that America's National Security Agency (the NSA) was collecting vast amounts of data under the pretence of fighting terrorism. In reality, much of the data collected had nothing at all to do with terrorist suspects but rather with advancing political agendas. In other words, this mass surveillance is not entirely about security – it's also about power.

Even if increased surveillance is genuinely well intentioned, there must be some accountability, or else the door is opened to a wide range of potential abuses. For example, personal information can be leaked to sabotage political rivals or used for blackmail. Even if we (very optimistically) assume that everyone in the government is incorruptible, the rate of cyber security breaches is increasing with each passing year. If private data are not used by bad actors within the government, the risk of hackers obtaining and abusing data is also very real.

Freedom of Expression

Farhan's story illustrates something of how cryptocurrency and blockchains can help to secure the freedom of information. This freedom can be a powerful bulwark against repressive governments. But it's not only governments that we have to worry about – corporations also have a growing power over society.

An increasing number of reports claim that social media content is being moderated based on the biases of the platforms. Right-leaning activists have complained of their posts being deleted or *shadow-banned* while left-wing activists expressing opinions that violate the terms of service go unchecked on sites like Twitter and Facebook. Since these platforms are based in California – an area noted for its liberal political leanings – some have suggested that employees are manipulating public discourse to promote their personal views.

Whether these allegations are accurate or not, the otential for this type of abuse clearly exists. The prospect of immutable data storage has also raised hopes of censorship-proof media.

Prototypes already exist for censorship-proof social media platforms based on blockchain technology. The most well-known of these is Steemit, a blockchain-based blogging platform. But such platforms raise the question about speech that crosses the boundaries of morality or legality. For example, Facebook now has thousands of dedicated staff who work full time to take down content that includes extreme violence, hateful views or pornographic imagery.

It is, however, possible to address these problems without relying on a centralised authority. Although public blockchains are open by nature, the applications used to interact with blockchains can be configured to block certain users or types of content. Think of it as the difference between the internet and a browser – you can't control what content appears on the internet, but you can adjust your browser settings.

And while there is a great deal of disturbing content on the internet, it can also make it easier for law enforcement to track and catch the people engaged in these activities. Additionally, some have argued that de-platforming extremists has led to further radicalisation, as this pushes them into forums and discussion groups where everyone shares their views. This amplifies extremist tendencies, while contact with opposing views that comes through participation in more open platforms can actually moderate these tendencies.

It's a difficult topic, and it's by no means a good thing to provide a platform for those sharing objectionable content. At the same time, it's a tragedy when the power of censorship is abused to limit the reach of individuals acting in the public interest. And there's a strong argument to be made for allowing open discussion of even the most abhorrent ideologies if only for the sake of resolving conflict through dialogue rather than isolation or violence.

Linguist and social critic Noam Chomsky summarised this discussion very succinctly when he said: "If we don't believe in freedom of expression for people we despise, then we don't believe in it at all."

The Importance of Decentralisation

Immutable data also has major implications for the way we view history, and this, in turn, can have a huge impact on politics. George Orwell once said: "Who controls the present controls the past, and who controls the past controls the future."

The censorship resistance of decentralised blockchains means that several important details are guaranteed beyond a shadow of a doubt when recorded on a blockchain:

- What was written
- Who wrote it
- When it was published

This could prevent, for example, a regime from trying to erase documentation of a genocide. On a more mundane level, it could prevent bad actors from producing fake news by imitating the logo of government or media agencies. Also very relevant in both the stories of Amadou and Farhan, blockchains allow the preservation of public financial records, which can give a major boost to transparency and trust in government.

Decentralisation is the only way to ensure that this immutability is preserved. The more centralised a blockchain becomes, the easier it is for the centralised authority to modify data. This is a factor that also points to the eventual convergence of cryptocurrencies to a single standard, which some believe will be Bitcoin. Since a cryptocurrency's valuation is dependent on its security, and security is proportional to the size of the network, Bitcoin has the highest utility, and thus the highest value. This value attracts more miners, which in turn increases the security further and further increases the value.

Given that this is such a threat to centralised power structures, it's not surprising that there are some very powerful advocates of centralised blockchains as well. Several governments, as well as many players in the banking industry, have embraced centralised blockchains. Chinese President Xi Jinping made blockchain development a core part of a five-year plan, calling on the nation to take a *leading stance* on blockchain development. This strategy makes sense and is consistent with China's approach to the internet so far. Instead of using Google, for example, China developed its own alternative, Baidu. Likewise, Facebook is blocked by the Great Firewall, but WeChat has proved a popular alternative. In this same spirit, China is already moving to create a central-bank-issued cryptocurrency with *controllable anonymity*.

It appears that the strategy China has chosen to try to minimise the undesirable aspects of digital currency is to recognise the demand for this technology and provide as many of its benefits as possible without entirely relinquishing control. In this way, they can prevent the widespread adoption of more dangerous protocols.

These efforts notwithstanding, the presence of decentralised, immutable protocols has already enabled several activists to circumvent government censorship. For example, one Peking University student published a letter exposing the university's efforts to cover up sexual misconduct on the part of a professor. After evidence was posted online, the letter was deleted several times by the authorities. Finally, the student posted the letter to the Ethereum blockchain, thus rendering it undeletable. In another case, Chinese citizens used a decentralised blockchain to preserve documentation that a company had faked the efficacy of more than 100,000 vaccines.

The concern is that government powers are sometimes used to protect business interests that run contrary to the interests of the people. While some of the most ardent cryptocurrency advocates are anarchists and libertarians that reject the notion of government entirely, in reality, these technologies could improve the function of governments.

In many cases, bad actors within governments remain unknown even to their colleagues. All too often, those in positions of authority use their power to cover up evidence that could expose their corruption. Better privacy and integrity of data can empower not only citizens but also workers within governments to increase the accountability of corporations and institutions.

When Edward Snowden blew the whistle on the NSA's vast spying operations, he had to use Bitcoin to pay for the server he used to store the leaked data. He knew that if he used his bank or credit card to pay, his employer could get wind of what he was up to and arrest him.

WikiLeaks was forced to look into accepting donations in Bitcoin after PayPal, under government pressure, froze their account in 2010. At the time, Satoshi Nakamoto pleaded with the WikiLeaks team to give them more time to develop the software, concerned that association with WikiLeaks would damage the reputation of Bitcoin and cause a negative reaction to the project. WikiLeaks agreed and delayed accepting donations in Bitcoin until 2011.

Some critics believe that Snowden and Wikileaks are treacherous or dangerous and endanger the lives of military personnel. Others regard them as a necessary check against egregious violations on the part of governments. Ultimately, however, almost everyone can agree that more government accountability is a good thing, and it's clear that cryptocurrency is a powerful tool in the hands of activists and journalists who might otherwise be censored, arrested, or even killed.

Pooling the Power of the People

Before the rise of decentralised currency, the internet already had major implications for activists around the world. Encryption has allowed undercover journalists living in totalitarian regimes to expose abuses of power. Social media enables the oppressed to get their message out to the world. But all of this has only been concerned with information.

The ability to access funding is essential to organising a cohesive social movement. With the rise of cryptocurrency, it is possible for organisations operating under totalitarian regimes to run their finances without fear of their funds being seized. A worldwide network would have the unprecedented ability to deploy money wherever its most pressing needs might be. In Farhan's case, he networked with other Iranian journalists in exile who were also actively exposing corruption within the government.

Farhan's story had a happy ending, but many stories of journalists and civil rights activists around the world do not end so well. However, money that is easier to access can enable more open dialogue, and if journalists and activists are freer to operate, individuals will have more chances to air their grievances and expose abuse. This expanded dialogue could greatly help to resolve conflicts without violence.

Amadou's story touched on how blockchain technology could bring more transparency to national elections, but consider how this could impact stateless groups. Bloody conflicts like the Basque and Northern Irish independence movements, as well as dozens of other regional conflicts around the world, are ultimately about a people's right to self-determination and autonomy.

By allowing for more autonomy in finances, these groups may be able to achieve a greater degree of political independence without needing to resort to violence. The movement towards a currency that is outside the control of conventional political authorities could enable humanity to evolve beyond territorial conflicts. The increasing digitisation of the economy means that economic power, and thus political authority, will be more and more virtual as time goes on.

We can certainly hope that this will allow people belonging to different identity groups to coexist in the same space more harmoniously. The robust and open dialogue that cryptocurrency enables will be the cornerstone of any development of this nature.

6. Chaturi Jayartne

When Opportunity Meets Talent

Chaturi Jayartne was the youngest of seven siblings. Her family lived in a very humble shack that her father had pieced together over the years by collecting corrugated roofing, plywood and canvas sheeting reclaimed from old advertising billboards. It was one of many such houses in the neighbourhood of Wanathamulla on the outskirts of Colombo, Sri Lanka. Many called the neighbourhood a slum. For Chaturi, it was home.

It was all she ever knew, so she never thought there was anything odd about the stench of open sewers or cats scavenging through heaps of garbage in the streets. Chaturi was a bright and happy girl, and she thought having dirty water and getting sick from time to time was just the natural order of things.

Her father had died of typhoid when she was five years old, and her mother worked twelve hours a day, six days a week, in a nearby garment factory to support the family. Her oldest sister took care of the younger children while their mother was at work. To help make ends meet, the family ran a small shop in the form of a table set up in front of the house selling odds and ends like rice and packets of laundry soap.

When she was eight, her oldest brother, Sandun, borrowed some money from a relative to pay an employment broker to get him a job as a construction worker in Dubai. Each month, he would send around 20,000 Sri Lankan rupees to his family, the equivalent of about 80 British pounds. With this extra income, the family could afford to send two of the siblings to school. Chaturi very much wanted to go, but she knew that as the youngest girl in the family, she didn't stand a chance.

However, she was still very interested in the process of her brothers going to school. Each day she waited anxiously for them to come home, and as soon as they arrived, she enquired about everything they'd learned. When they went out to play football, she scanned their books and notebooks and traced the letters in the dirt floor of their home with a stick, teaching herself to read and write.

Around the age of twelve, she found work not far from home washing clothes. Most of her earnings went towards paying the family's daily living expenses, but she used some to expand the stock of the family shop. When her duties were over at work, she came home to tend the shop and was always looking for ways to increase the takings so that she could make a better life for the family.

She would watch her customers' eyes when they came to make a purchase and then rearrange her wares so that they would be more likely to catch their attention. While walking around the neighbourhood fetching water or purchasing supplies, she would ask other shop owners about the prices of all of their goods and make mental notes.

The shop's earnings gradually increased, and life got a bit better. They were eating well at last, but they still couldn't afford to pay Chaturi's school fees. On top of that, her oldest sister got married and moved out. And with her two older brothers busy at school, she was left to look after the shop on her own. She resolved to devote all of her considerable mental energy and talents to the shop.

As bright as she was, it was tough to get ahead. The people in the neighbourhood simply didn't have the money to spend, so although she developed very sharp business acumen, it made little difference to the family's situation. They were surviving, but not much more than that.

She couldn't go to school, but she was still desperate to learn. On her trips to the market, she would collect scraps of discarded newspaper, which she would read while waiting for customers. She became a skilled and meticulous bookkeeper, and like many teenage girls, began to keep a journal. She borrowed every book she could but never felt she had enough to read.

She had played around on her friends' phones, and while they were mainly interested in social media or chatting, she realised you could download all kinds of texts and was determined to get a phone of her own. Finally, after saving for the better part of a year, she had enough for an HTC mobile at around 25,000 rupees – little more than 100 pounds, but a small fortune for Chaturi's family.

Her new phone soon became her most prized possession. She could rarely afford to pay for internet credit, but the family she worked for gave her the password to their Wi-Fi. Most of the kids in her neighbourhood used their internet access to watch Bollywood movies and music videos, but for some reason, Chaturi was different.

After work, she would download books, videos and audio lectures before she went home. When she got home to tend the shop, she would go through all the materials she'd downloaded. One could hardly imagine a more disadvantaged situation, but she used her abundance of free time to her advantage and gave herself an even better education than her brothers were getting in school.

She had put so much thought into finding ways to better support her family through the shop that she now knew a lot about business. As her English improved, she downloaded lectures from Oxford, MIT, Harvard and Stanford and explored topics like business logic, machine learning, and behavioural economics. She read the biographies of Warren Buffett and Steve Jobs and learned that HTC, the company that manufactured her beloved phone, was co-founded by a woman, Cher Wang.

On the outside, she looked just like any other girl – keeping her humble shop, staring at the screen of her mobile phone. Like many girls her age, she also enjoyed playing games on her phone. She started out playing Theme Park Tycoon and amassed a virtual fortune. Then, based on recommendations in the Google Play store, she downloaded a stock market trading simulator and also did quite well on that.

The more she learned, the more the family business thrived. Under her watch, the shop had grown, and now she was selling phone credit as well and could stay online even while she was watching the shop.

In the chatbox of one of her favourite stock market simulators, she overheard other players talking about trading on decentralised exchanges. She had made lots of money in the simulator, *so why not try trading with real money?* she thought. She decided to give it a go. She found a website that gave out tiny amounts of Bitcoin in exchange for watching advertisements. After watching several hundred videos, she collected enough Bitcoin to make a deposit and start investing.

The exchange where she created her account had several tokens that represented real-world stocks along with property, commodities, and equity in early-stage tech startups. Even though she only had a few thousand rupees, she tried to apply some of the investment strategies she'd heard about in her studies, hedging risks and balancing her portfolio. She also looked at other exchanges, searching for lower trade fees.

In the process, she noticed differences in the prices of some crypto assets and saw arbitrage opportunities. She began transferring small amounts of money back and forth between the different exchanges, making a few rupees after fees on each trade.

Whenever she saw different companies trading on the exchanges, she would read about them, looking for sound fundamentals. At one point, she stumbled across an Indian startup that had developed an innovative portable wastewater treatment system. Having grown up around raw sewage, she immediately recognised the value of such a solution. After investigating the profiles of the founders and finding the results impressive, she decided to invest some of her savings in the company.

Her investments in property, gold and cryptocurrency continued to appreciate gradually, and her steady profits in arbitrage also added to her growing wealth. At times, she made mistakes – one bad arbitrage deal could erase weeks of progress, but she was careful always to make notes of her mistakes and how she could avoid them in the future.

She also studied the news, looking for opportunities. When she read about turmoil in the European Union, she thought to herself that if she were a wealthy European, she would probably invest in property in relatively stable markets in the Caribbean. So she moved some of her wealth into a Caribbean-based property trust.

After several years like this, she had learned a tremendous amount, and found that her few thousand rupees had turned into more than 30,000. She'd hardly been paying attention to the overall value of her portfolio – it was more of a hobby than anything else, a way to pass the time when waiting for customers to come to the shop.

Then she received word that the startup she'd invested in had been purchased by a major corporation at a significant mark-up. This windfall yielded a handsome profit, more than doubling the total value of her portfolio. She considered buying a new phone but decided against it and reinvested everything.

Her positive experience with equity financing saw her focusing more on tech startups. She also bought into several funds specialising in early-stage tech equity and, in a few very promising cases, bought shares herself. She understood very well that it was a higher risk profile, so she was careful to keep her portfolio balanced and diversified. She even invested in residential property crowd-financing in the UK.

She had a string of failures after her first success, investing in companies that went bankrupt, but overall, she managed to realise gains despite the losses. She also deepened her knowledge of what to look out for before investing in growth-stage companies.

Meanwhile, she had been steadily accumulating cryptocurrency to increase her arbitrage earnings. When a major shock hit the foreign exchange market, her cryptocurrency holdings tripled in value in a matter of weeks. She decided to capitalise on the panic and began using her cryptocurrency profits to buy up equity in distressed companies with sound fundamentals in Europe, Japan and North America.

Around this time, her brother, Sandun, returned from working abroad. He'd changed a lot while he'd been away and was planning to use his savings to finally marry. To do this, he wanted to demolish their shack and build a proper house. Chaturi was almost 19, and he decided there would be no room for her in the new house. It was time for her to marry.

Chaturi wasn't opposed to marrying, but she'd been so focused on her virtual business world she'd hardly had time to think about it. When Sandun introduced her to his friend Nuwan, she was initially open to the idea. He seemed very nice and certainly handsome. Her brother recommended him highly, pointing out that he owned three rickshaws. One thing that troubled her a little was that he always had a cigarette in his mouth. And when a friend mentioned he was always getting into fights when he was younger, her uneasiness increased.

On Nuwan's third visit, she asked if he'd ever thought about quitting smoking, saying she was concerned about his health. His charm disappeared, and his eyes flashed with anger.

"Who are you to tell me what to do?" he asked.

She didn't press the issue, but from the way he talked to her, she knew she didn't want to marry him. After Nuwan left, Chaturi told Sandun how she felt, and he was enraged.

"Most girls in your position would be thrilled to have a husband like Nuwan! You should be grateful."

Chaturi explained her reservations. Sandun was indignant.

"You're 19 years old. It's time for you to marry, and I can't have you hanging around the house forever. If you turn down this opportunity, we don't know when there will be another."

Sandun was firm. Chaturi was to marry Nuwan. Chaturi insisted that she had cared for the family's shop and that with the income the shop was bringing in, she was no load on the family. Sandun didn't see it that way. His new wife could tend the shop just as well, he said.

Her mother pleaded with Sandun to no avail. He insisted that she was to marry Nuwan.

Chaturi had seen several of her friends in similar situations, trapped in unhappy marriages. She liquidated a percentage of her portfolio and took the difficult decision to leave home.

Her family was shocked. How would she survive on her own? She had spent a lot of time on her phone, but that wasn't at all unusual for girls her age in their neighbourhood. They had no idea that she'd been accumulating real wealth. Her mother wept as Chaturi's packed her things and left. Chaturi reassured her that she'd still be nearby, renting a room not far from her work.

Freed from her household duties of washing, cleaning, and tending the shop, she poured all her energy into studying and improving her online investments, making major gains. Within a year, she had several hundred thousand rupees. She had already spent years running a shop and understood the market very well, and she noticed some gaps. She liquidated a little more of her portfolio and opened a shop of her own. To have more time to focus on research and investments, she hired her older sister to work there.

Contrary to what Sandun had thought, Chaturi had been contributing quite a lot to the household. Now that she was no longer supporting the family with her work in the shop, she began to reinvest the profits instead, adding further momentum to her investments. By the time she was 22, she had expanded the offering of her first shop and opened a second. What's more, she still had enough funds to invest in tech startups in various markets around the world.

She soon became known as the most successful businesswoman in Wanathamulla, and as she was also young, many young men approached her with proposals of marriage.

One of them was a quiet boy she'd seen occasionally walking back and forth in front of her old house. His name was Chamath, and he'd just graduated from college and started working as a history teacher at the nearby school. He told her he'd been infatuated with her for years, but when he told his mother that he wished to marry her, she was violently against the notion of her son marrying a poor washing girl. But now, with Chaturi's exceptional success well known around the neighbourhood, his mother had changed her tune and was right behind the idea.

Chamath visited Chaturi several times, and with each visit, it became increasingly clear that he was kind and had genuine affection for her, unlike many of her other suitors, who were a little too interested in her money. She spoke with her very supportive mother, who knew Chamath's family and thought he would be an excellent match.

Sri Lankan wedding tradition called for a somewhat elaborate ceremony with the construction of a decorative wooden platform where the bride and groom would sit during the wedding ritual. They also had to pay for decorations, the rental of the venue, along with traditional costumes and jewellery and entertainment for the guests. It was customary for the bride's family to cover all expenses, but Sandun was still angry about Chaturi's refusal to marry Nuwan and refused to support her in any way.

Many of Chaturi and Chamath's friends had to delay marriage for years or go deeply into debt to pay for their wedding, but thanks to Chaturi's financial success, the young couple broke with tradition and shared the expense.

After what everyone agreed was a marvellous ceremony, Sandun grudgingly approached Chaturi to congratulate her.

"I'm very happy for you. I wish you many blessings in your marriage," he said.

"Thank you, brother," she replied. "That's very kind."

"Chaturi, I wanted to say something to you. I'm very sorry about... before... I didn't mean to hurt your feelings."

"That's alright. I'm doing fine, brother."

"I wanted to talk to you about the shop. It hasn't been doing so well since you left. I don't know why, but we've been losing money. Is there any way you could loan me 100,000 rupiahs?"

Chaturi wanted to laugh, but she managed to keep her composure. She thought about it for a moment and replied.

"Well, brother, I wouldn't want you to be burdened with debt. How about you sell me the shop for 100,000 rupiahs, and I'll pay you 4,000 rent each month." It was a very generous offer, and he happily accepted. She knew she was overpaying, but she also knew she wouldn't lose money on the deal. And she was happy to support her family.

Chaturi moved in with Chamuth's family, and the young couple's marriage started very happily. But soon, Chamath's mother began to criticise Chaturi.

"That girl does nothing all day but sit on her phone. And you've been married for four months now, and she's still not pregnant!" Chamath tried to defend her, explaining that she was working and pursuing her passion. But it seemed his mother retained her prejudices against Chaturi's humble background.

The couple decided they'd have to move out to escape the continual criticism. They could easily have afforded to move to a better neighbourhood, but Chaturi wanted to stay close to her family, friends, and her shops. She also wanted to use her success to help her community rather than escape from it like so many others, and she already employed several girls whose lives had been improved by the job opportunities she'd given them. So the young couple rented an apartment across the street from Chaturi's first shop.

One day, the Indian startup she'd invested in announced it would soon be exporting its portable wastewater treatment units, and Chaturi had an idea. She already had significant cryptocurrency holdings accumulated from years of arbitrage, investing and saving, and one of the units cost just over one million rupiahs. She knew it would be a risky venture but calculated that if she used her cryptocurrency as collateral, she had enough income to pay off the loan even if it didn't work out. She also thought it was likely that her cryptocurrency reserves would continue appreciating, and in her studies, she'd learned that it's wise to put as much of your capital to work as possible.

Chamath had an uncle in the urban development department who helped them obtain the necessary permits, and Chaturi deposited the collateral online and got the loan. She contacted an import broker, submitted the order, and waited anxiously for the unit to arrive. In the meantime, she spoke with her neighbours and the community elders, and they all agreed that she could place the unit in a free area next to a stagnant open sewage canal. She also contacted several nurseries in the more upscale neighbourhoods of Colombo and inquired about their fertilizer needs.

The unit, when it arrived, looked very humble – it resembled a small shipping container. The novel method of wastewater treatment involved electrocoagulation. The treatment units used electrical current rather than chemistry to break down the chemical bonds in the waste and accelerate its decomposition. Soon, the unit was processing over 20,000 litres of wastewater a day and yielding usable fertilizer.

Chaturi found two nurseries willing to buy, and an uncle of Chamath's, who owned a sandalwood plantation in the countryside, also agreed to buy some of the fertilizer. These contracts alone were enough to cover the operating costs, but there was still an excess of fertilizer.

Chaturi struggled to find buyers. She was barely breaking even, and she knew she needed to find a market in order to turn a profit. If she could just find some product that was in demand, she thought, and produce it herself, it would be much easier than trying to capture market share in the local fertilizer market.

She remembered investing in a number of small projects that had sold shares in their equipment via tokens. In line with the philosophy of putting all of her capital to work, she realised she could raise more money by tokenising the waste processing unit and selling shares in it. She gathered all of the documentation on the venture, drafted a contract, had it notarised, and uploaded it to a crypto financing platform in the form of a smart contract.

Dividend-paying shares representing a 50 per cent stake in the waste processing unit were issued. Since she already had proven cash flow, the tokens sold quickly. Chaturi set about putting her plan into action. When purchasing decorations for their wedding, Chaturi had been struck by the high price of cut flowers. After researching the industry in other countries, it seemed to her that the cost of labour and production inputs in Sri Lanka was quite reasonable, and when she ran her calculations, it looked like it would be profitable.

With the funds from the token sale, she purchased some materials to build a greenhouse. Chamath's uncle who ran the sandalwood plantation was an agricultural engineer, and he travelled to Colombo to help them set up the operation. The climate of Sri Lanka was very well suited to growing roses, and the first harvest was ready within three months.

They found a few shops willing to purchase the flowers in Colombo, but the real success came when Sanduk visited Chaturi again, asking to borrow more money. Instead of the loan, she offered him a job in the greenhouse. He happily agreed, and when he told her more about the work, he remembered something.

"You know, when I was working in Dubai, there was a flower shop near our apartment. A friend of mine worked there, and he told me people used to come in and spend more money on a bouquet than our monthly salaries combined! Why don't I call some of my friends over there and see if they know any buyers?"

Chaturi excitedly agreed. Two days later, one of Sanduk's friends called back to say he'd spoken with a distributor who was willing to pay half a dirham per rose for a shipment of 1,000 roses. Chaturi pulled up the calculator on her phone. Half a dirham was about 25 rupees. She contacted an air freight agent and then factored in the transport costs. The profit margin, after all the expenses, was approximately ten per cent.

Weekly shipments began soon after, and she started to pay off the initial loan. At the same time, she set aside profits for future expansion. She began calling other distributors and secured another contract about six months later. By optimising the timing of the shipments and improving production at the greenhouse, she succeeded in lowering costs and increasing the profit margin.

By the time she freed up her collateral from the first loan, it had increased in value even more. She used it again to take out a bigger loan to purchased two more wastewater treatment units and expand the greenhouse. She hired more of her friends, and soon, thanks to the improved wages in the neighbourhood, rusty corrugated steel walls were replaced with plywood sheets painted bright pink, teal, and blue. The portable waste treatment units were processing the majority of the sewage in the neighbourhood, and the ever-present stench of sewage began to fade.

Much to her mother-in-law's delight, Chaturi announced that she was pregnant. As the delivery date approached, Chamath left his job to help his wife with the greenhouses and exports. Up until the birth, Chaturi continued working the phones and searching for new clients and managed to secure new contracts in China and Italy.

The baby was born without complications. After three days, Chaturi and Chamath came home from the hospital. When she stepped out into the street, baby in arms, she paused for a moment. The neighbourhood was still rough around the edges, but it was much cleaner than she remembered from her own childhood. A faint scent of roses coming from the nearby greenhouse had replaced the stench of sewage. As her friends and neighbours came to congratulate her and take a peek at the new baby, it struck her that with the improving economic fortunes of the area, the whole mood seemed cheerier.

Once considered a slum that everyone wanted to escape from, Chaturi now saw the place as a friendly neighbourhood, where she would be happy and proud to raise her children.

***

The Financial Centre of the World

Most of us are familiar with some of the great financial centres of the world – New York, London, Hong Kong. Do you ever wonder why these cities became financial centres in the first place?

Well, you might be familiar with the concept of economies of scale, which says that products can often be produced more efficiently at a large scale. This is the logic of the assembly line. When it comes to competition, larger businesses can often offer products at a lower price than their smaller rivals because their production costs are lower. Likewise, transporting large quantities of goods is often cheaper than transporting smaller amounts.

This is precisely why such financial concentrations happened in the first place. By concentrating capital, investors can finance larger businesses that produce goods more efficiently.

The ability to concentrate money from diverse sources and channel it to good business opportunities is why the financial sector appeared. Larger concentrations of capital thus had an advantage over smaller concentrations, so financial institutions concentrated in small areas in order to finance bigger and more efficient businesses.

This situation is now changing. When businesses were still funded by gold coins, if you wanted to finance a large venture, you had to gather the required number of gold coins together in one physical location. Logistically, it was also necessary to be in the same city to meet with investors, borrowers, lawyers, and all of the various stakeholders that make successful business deals possible. Paperwork had to be shuffled around the city, and even now, bicycle couriers play an crucial role in many business districts.

One of the problems with this situation is the tendency to concentrate wealth. Since there was a comparative advantage in having more capital to work with, there is a tendency for the rich to get richer and the poor to get poorer. This has not only made some individuals absurdly rich – it has also contributed to inequality between countries.

Video conferencing, digital signatures, and most importantly, digital currencies are changing all of this. In the days of paper cheques, gold coins, and bicycle messengers carrying important documents around to be notarised, it made perfect sense to concentrate financial districts in the Square Mile or Wall Street. That's just not the case anymore. The internet is the new financial centre of the world, and it has the potential to be orders of magnitude more efficient than our legacy systems.

The creation of a borderless, world capital market accessible to all is one of the most obvious ways that cryptocurrency stands to disrupt the global financial order. While the implications for low-income countries are enormous, there are also many ways this paradigm shift can affect developed financial markets as well. One notable example is *sophisticated investor status*.

Sophisticated Investor Status

One of the main fears surrounding a free and open financial system is the risk of uneducated or unqualified retail investors suffering significant losses. This is certainly a valid concern. Both in traditional finance and in cryptocurrency, there have been many scams that have resulted in enormous losses for investors. For this reason, many countries have implemented regulations that prevent ordinary people from making certain kinds of investments.

These regulations usually limit who can invest in early-stage technology companies. This seems reasonable on the surface – after all, more than 90% of tech startups fail. So, what do you need to become an *accredited investor* in countries with such legislation?

Usually, it's a combination of one or more of the following:

- A high net worth
- A very high income
- Professional experience in the financial sector

For example, in Australia, you need a net worth of AUD 2,500,000 (~GBP 1.3 million) or an income of more than AUD 250,000 for the previous two years. In Canada, you'd need CAD 5,000,000 (~GBP 2.9 million). In the relatively lax European Union, you'll only need an investment portfolio exceeding 500,000 euros in value.

Ostensibly, this legislation is intended to protect investors. Yet, in most of the countries with laws like these, it's perfectly legal for you to take out a loan against your house and waste it all at the casino. In fact, many people do just that every year and end up financially ruined. So if it's the responsibility of governments to protect everyone, why aren't they running about shutting down casinos?

Whatever the answer to that question might be, it's clear that these regulations have another effect beyond just protecting investors. They limit investment opportunities for anyone who is not already rich. In other words, the rich get richer, and the poor get poorer.

Even despite these protections, so-called registered sophisticated investors also lose large amounts of money in scams – the most famous recent example being Bernie Madoff's multi-billion dollar Ponzi scheme.

No one is immune to making poor investment choices. Even the best, most well-educated traders are sometimes ruined by so-called *black swan* events – rare occurrences that are impossible to predict. No matter how robust a risk management strategy is, the inescapable reality is that there can be no profit without some level of risk. Some people may be protected by these regulations, but it also harms many others who are denied great investment opportunities.

So how exactly does cryptocurrency open up these opportunities? How can it help brilliant individuals like Chaturi to access opportunities that would have never before been accessible?

The answer lies in technology as well as law. As described in Chapter 3, distributed, blockchain-based networks make it possible to create secure digital tokens with a set number of units. This allows for the issuance of ownership shares in just about anything – from a company to property or even a decentralised network.

But the law can be used to provide access to opportunities that were previously limited to very few individuals. For example, let's imagine the dream scenario – a tech unicorn-like Facebook.

If you'd invested in Facebook's initial public offering in 2012, you'd have done alright seven years later. Facebook shares are up approximately 400% since the IPO. But this is nothing compared to the profits of seed round investors. Peter Thiel invested USD 500,000 in 2004, purchasing approximately 10% of the young company. He liquidated these shares in the period following the IPO, netting a cool USD one billion – or a 200,000% profit.

Stories like these are why venture capital funds are still able to make money, even though the majority of the companies they invest in fail. Indeed, analysis and savvy have a lot to do with success at investing, but no one can deny that there is also some element of dumb luck.

With the rise of decentralised blockchains, some firms are exploiting legal loopholes to enable retail investors to circumvent sophisticated investor regulations. It works more or less like this: a registered financial company purchases a stake in a tech startup that is only available to sophisticated investors. The company then issues tokens on a blockchain that represent this ownership stake in a jurisdiction where such token issuance is legal and then sells the tokens online for cryptocurrency.

The link between these tokens and the actual investment in the startup is backed by a legal guarantee and a real company, so in effect, ordinary people around the world are able to access investments that were once limited to the ultra-wealthy in advanced financial markets.

This may be prohibited in the US or the UK, but the governments of those countries are only responsible for protecting their own citizens – if that's what these laws are really about. Regardless of whether sophisticated investor status laws are really about protecting people or there is a sinister ulterior motive to give an unfair advantage to the rich, these regulations will very soon become impossible to enforce.

All of this links to the discussion about cryptocurrency fraud in Chapter 3. Regulators must recognise their limitations and move resources instead towards educating the public about the dangers of these new technologies. Countries that move to guide their citizens in profiting from this technology will have an advantage over those that attempt to hold onto antiquated regulatory regimes.

Many countries are already moving to boost their finances by attracting startups in the cryptocurrency space. In 2017, Malta fully legalised and regulated cryptocurrencies and tokens and branded itself as *Blockchain Island*. If the trend of decentralisation of the financial system continues, such forward-thinking countries are likely to become leaders in the coming transformation.

Don't Beggar Thy Neighbour

It's natural to fear the unknown. Cryptocurrency is just one factor of many changing the boundaries that define the modern world. And, for a lot of people, these changes are quite scary. Many fear that if money is set free, jobs will go international, opportunity will be more evenly distributed, and there will be a reduction in the wealth of countries like the UK.

The idea of wealth becoming more distributed is frightening to some people. It's logical on the surface to think that fewer capital controls might lead to lower wages. This is because it seems that if wealth is more evenly shared, it could mean a reduction in wealth for those of us who live in relatively wealthy countries. In other words, if the minimum wage in England is £8 per hour, and the minimum wage in Angola is £0.80 per hour, and we imagine that wealth and opportunities were distributed equally between the two countries, it would mean that the minimum wage for both countries would be £4.40.

This thinking drives so-called *beggar-thy-neighbour* policies, which promote the economic interests of one country at the expense of others. These fears are unfounded, and this is not how the economy works. Excessive concentration of wealth actually results in drastically reduced productivity, which means less wealth for everyone. This is because people with no money don't buy anything. In other words, ten people with a million pounds each will generate much more economic activity than one person with ten million pounds.

The success of many businesses in the UK, for example, is limited by how many buyers there are for their products. If the level of wealth increased in impoverished countries, so too would the number of buyers in those countries. This would translate into more business opportunities, more jobs, and higher wages.

There are many other ways that the world would actually benefit from the more balanced distribution of wealth that free, open money enables. As barriers to trade lower, the total amount of wealth produced by the world economy increases. In economics, this is known as the law of comparative advantage. With greater specialisation comes greater efficiency. If you spend more time doing a particular kind of work, you're going to become better at it. In other words, a jack-of-all-trades will usually be a master of none.

A freer economic system can also unlock hidden potential around the world. The story of Chaturi is meant to illustrate how the opportunities once unique to major financial centres are now opening to anyone with enough intelligence, motivation, and an internet connection. This is not just about helping the poor – it's about helping everyone.

Around the world, there are individuals with incredible talent who have the potential to be the next generation of leaders, scientists, inventors and entrepreneurs. If they never have the means to use and cultivate their talents, the whole of humanity loses out. Cryptocurrency opens doors for brilliant individuals to realise their potential for the benefit of humankind. Chaturi had a brilliant analytical ability and a keen sense for business and investment. Although she lived in a slum in Sri Lanka, cryptocurrency gave her the same access to opportunity that anyone in London, Hong Kong, or New York might have.

Another critical aspect that is often forgotten in economic analysis is the cost of the social tension that results from a lack of economic opportunities. For one, poverty leads to corruption. Naturally, if a police officer or a government official has a salary of £200 per month, they'll be much more likely to accept bribes. Both corruption and extreme inequality lead to violence and conflict. This may be lovely for the arms industry, but the arms industry is a relatively small portion of economic output, even for weapon producing behemoths like the United States or Russia.

How much value is lost every year to corruption, war, and poverty? How much talent goes wasted for lack of opportunity? And how much could world economic output be improved by free and open finance?

Numerous researchers have discovered a link between a lack of economic opportunities and extremism and terrorism. What if, instead of dumping billions into endless wars that seem to aggravate the problem, we put more energy into creating more opportunities, addressing inequality, and increasing the overall wellbeing of everyone?

7. Dwayne Henry

Money for Peace

Like many veterans of war, Dwayne Henry was a haunted man – an all-too-common example of a soldier struggling with the transition back to civilian life. He thought that the sense of dread and emptiness inside him would go away when he returned to his hometown in Minnesota after his second tour of duty. He was happy to see his family and friends, but somehow he felt as if he was outside his body, watching his own life as an independent observer. Sometimes he felt that he couldn't feel anything at all anymore.

When he did feel something, it was usually fear, anxiety, and remorse. After a few days back home, however, he found that if he drank enough beer, he could forget his pain and even have a few laughs with his friends, just like old times. But he soon found himself chasing that feeling, and a few drinks at the weekend soon turned into a nightly ritual.

Part of the reason he drank was just to sleep. On some nights, he couldn't sleep at all. Other nights, he fell asleep shortly after going to bed, only to wake up, alert, after an hour. The worst nights were the ones where the nightmares came to him. Whisky was the one way to guarantee the nightmares wouldn't come.

Of the many horrors he'd witnessed during the war, one day in particular was burned into his memory. It had started out like any other. They were setting up a new checkpoint. Dwayne and his commanding officer had stopped with their translator to ask a street vendor to move his cart. Dwayne scanned the road, searching for possible threats. Further down, local partner forces were redirecting traffic. Suddenly, Dwayne heard shouting and was instantly alert.

A dilapidated blue Fiat had ignored a command to halt and broken through the cordon into the street. Dwayne lifted his rifle and, almost as a reflex, fired a warning shot in front of the car, but it kept moving. His squad vehicle, with his friends and colleagues, was directly in the path of the car. A month earlier, his friend, Jim, had been killed when a suicide car bomber rammed his convoy. So Dwayne was acutely aware of the danger. The car didn't appear to be accelerating, but neither was it stopping. With no time to think, he had to act to protect the lives of his unit. He raised his aim and fired two three-shot salvos through the driver's side windshield.

The car didn't stop but instead veered to the right and smashed into a shopfront. In the heat of the moment, he felt himself shaking with adrenaline. Then he heard the screams – screams that would echo in his memory for years to come.

Dwayne and his unit didn't approach the car; instead, they called the ordnance disposal squad. A crowd emerged from the neighbouring buildings and gathered around the vehicle. They were still at least thirty paces away from Dwayne and his unit, but he could feel the glares of hatred. As they pulled the body of the driver from the car, he saw the source of the cries: a young girl, no older than five or six, clutching the bloodied, lifeless body of her father. Some of the crowd tried to pull her off, but she clung to the body, and her screams grew louder and more desperate.

Later, back at the base, as Dwayne filled out an incident report, it became clear what had happened. The old car's brakes had failed, and the driver, an impoverished schoolteacher, had swerved to avoid hitting a crowd of pedestrians and, in the process, crashed through the barrier. Witnesses said he'd been trying to yell an explanation, but it had all happened too fast.

The inspector's report confirmed that Dwayne had done nothing wrong – he'd done everything by the book. Though his commanding officer comforted him and put him in touch with the regimental psychologist, nothing could remove the sound of the little girl's cries from his mind.

It wasn't always the girl that kept him up at night. But the nights when he did see and hear her were the worst. Sometimes he saw her in his dreams, and sometimes he saw her standing next to the bed. Sometimes she was covered in blood, others she wasn't, but she was always screaming. He could close his eyes, cover his ears, or hide under the blanket, but he couldn't stop the screams.

The insomnia left him in a haze, a sort of purgatory, neither alive nor dead. The sleeping pills they gave him at the vets' hospital only left him feeling like he'd traded one haze for another. Whisky seemed to be the only thing that really worked. He was also prescribed painkillers for the chronic pain in his shoulder, the result of carrying heavy loads of weapons and ammunition. A mixture of liquor and painkillers was his go-to medication, though his doctor had warned him against it.

His son was barely walking, and his daughter was a newborn when Dwayne was first deployed. He scarcely recognised the kids when he came home, but he loved them very much, and seeing them was the best part of being back. Still, between his anxiety, medications, and sleep deprivation, he felt he wasn't a very good father to them. He would go to the lake or the park with them, and in the middle of playing, he would go blank and begin staring off into the distance, unresponsive until his wife or children brought him back to reality by physically shaking him.

His drinking got worse and worse and worse. Less than a year and a half after coming home, he would often be drunk by early afternoon when the kids got back from school. On other days, they'd find him unconscious and stinking of booze, sometimes on the couch and occasionally sprawled across the floor. His wife, Sandra, watched his suffering and felt powerless to do anything. Visits to therapists and treatment programs provided temporary relief, but after a few weeks, he always settled back into the same pattern.

His drinking and depression descended into a vicious downward spiral. Thanks to his military disability pension, he didn't need to work, but he desperately wanted a job and felt useless when he couldn't find one. His training came back to him, and he began to express his anger with violence. One night, he smashed a lamp against the wall. A few weeks later, the television fell victim to a spontaneous outburst. Then it was a window.

After each episode, he always apologised to Sandra once he sobered up and replaced or repaired whatever he'd broken. But one day, when she confronted him about his drinking, he went too far and became violent with her as well. When he sobered up, he hardly remembered what had happened, but he saw that her left eye was swollen and purple, and she was packing her things. He couldn't blame her, and he didn't even protest when she took the children. He didn't want them to see him like this.

Like many of his brothers in arms, he contemplated suicide. His family would be better off without him, he thought – without the shame of a broken father and husband. He would set his Smith and Wesson .357 revolver on the coffee table and stare at it, seeing if he could find the courage to go through with it. But there was something deep inside him that stopped him from ending it all.

Even if it meant suffering anxiety or seeing the visions that haunted him, he managed to stay sober at least one day a week to visit the children. He'd take them to the playground and sometimes have an ice cream afterwards. As he watched his son play, he sometimes thought to himself, "What if he ends up like me?"

This started him thinking about how he'd got to where he was today. He began to reflect on his life. He'd been a normal, happy youth in high school. How did he become such a broken alcoholic? When he first enlisted, he really believed he was going to defend his country and make the world a better place. In the course of his training, though, he learned to stop asking questions and to blindly follow orders. He learned to switch off his critical thinking, but no one had taught him how to shut off his conscience.

When he was first deployed, he uncritically accepted the explanations on the news. They were going to remove a brutal dictator, help a struggling nation transition to democracy, and ensure peace and stability in the region. All of this was essential to protect the peace and stability of America, he was assured.

Once he was on the ground, however, he started to see things that made him question this story. He saw their local partners using the weapons the American military provided them with to brutally repress rival tribes while his commanding officers turned a blind eye. After a while, he noticed that many of his patrols involved protecting the personnel and equipment of oil companies, while the oppressed people he thought he was there to help were living in dire poverty.

He started to research the events that had led up to the war. Oddly enough, he found his ever-present anxiety would subside when he watched documentaries or read about it. He still relied on whisky and pain pills to sleep, but he found he no longer needed to drink himself into unconsciousness. In the course of his research, he began watching videos on YouTube about the history of US military interventions. He watched former President Eisenhower's speech in which he warned Americans about *the military-industrial complex* and the danger of wars for profit. This led him to read about the long history of corporate influence on the American military.

Eventually, he stumbled on a theory that suggested the US dollar was used as a tool for projecting political influence. He began to suspect that what he'd been fighting for was a lie.

He couldn't shake the impression that he'd been used and thrown away. When he was on active duty, he'd always been busy following orders or trying to survive, but as a civilian, he had no sense of purpose. As he learned more and more about the causes of the war that had left him so scarred, he felt that sense of purpose slowly returning to him.

He came to believe that he had been manipulated and deceived, and he was filled with a powerful mixture of emotions. He was angry, but at the same time, he felt a great love. He was angry that he, his fellow soldiers, and their families had made so many sacrifices and caused pain and suffering on the basis of false pretexts. At the same time, he felt an urgent need to ensure that his children did not suffer the same fate. Even if he never became whole again, even if he was a shame to his family, he thought, he still had to do whatever he could to right the wrongs that he had helped commit.

He decided to make use of his veteran scholarship and enrolled in the local community college. At first, he just wanted to learn more about the topics he had started to explore on YouTube. He wanted to learn how to make a difference. He studied psychology and learned about PTSD and its treatments. He took a political science course, and he began to understand the responsibility of the media in a democratic society and how the American media had shirked that responsibility leading up to the war. He also enrolled in economics courses and started to better understand supply, demand, and inflation.

It all started to come together. He understood that he had not been sent to war to protect his people's freedoms – he'd been sent to protect the wealth of a small elite. At times it made him almost nauseous, but it also gave him hope. Now that he understood the problem, he could begin to look for the solution. Just as he had unconsciously been a tool for evil, he knew he could consciously become a force for good.

At the urging of his therapist, he began attending Alcoholics Anonymous. He'd tried in the past to go to meetings, but he had issues with anxiety around groups of people that made it very uncomfortable for him. But now, he felt eager to discuss his new knowledge with anyone he could. When he'd attended meetings in the past, he'd always dreaded it being his turn to talk. Now, he was eager to share how his sense of guilt and anxiety had driven him to alcohol. When he shared his thoughts out loud with the group, he realised that the path to overcoming his guilt and anxiety was to atone for the wrong he'd done. He found many sympathetic ears when discussing the ills of the country and the deception that had led them to war. It seemed that many people in his community were suffering from very similar problems.

When someone started discussing Bitcoin with him during a coffee break, he was immediately interested. He had heard so much about the US dollar being used as a tool for war that the idea of completely non-political currency intrigued him. From his studies at college, he was starting to understand that the financial system had contributed to the war in a number of ways, so the possibility of reforming the financial system seemed like it might be a way of avoiding future wars.

He also met a fellow veteran at the meeting who invited him to join an organisation called Veterans for Peace, where he met many others with stories similar to his own. He developed an especially strong bond with a man named Kurt, who had been stationed in the same city as Dwayne during the war.

In the spring, Kurt invited Dwayne to rent a plot in a nearby community garden. Working with the earth and watching the plants grow seemed to soothe his nerves. He also developed bonds with the other gardeners who shared advice on how best to care for his plants. During these discussions, he learned that many of them were growing food to gain more independence from the corporations that controlled their food supply and that those corporations were owned by the same people who owned the arms manufacturers that had lobbied for the war.

When he told his new friends about Bitcoin as a means of reducing support for the corporate and financial system, he found many open minds and ears. He convinced both the community garden association and Veterans for Peace to begin accepting donations in Bitcoin and became involved with fundraising efforts online.

Not everyone was receptive to his thinking, however. When he tried to tell his economics professor about Bitcoin, the response was very critical.

"Hah, a deflationary currency!" he scoffed. "That would lead to hoarding. Inflation is an incentive to spend." the professor explained.

Dwayne considered this. He was not necessarily opposed to inflation – he was opposed to inflation going into the hands of bankers and politicians, who, according to the YouTube channels he watched, also pushed for wars in order to gain more wealth and power. He saw Bitcoin as a superior way to save, but he also wondered what would happen if Bitcoin actually dethroned the dollar. If no one wanted to spend because the money was always going up in value, could a Bitcoin-based economy lead to mass unemployment?

For one of his group projects in economics, he partnered with a classmate, an awkward young man named Kevin. They got on very well with one another and became good friends. They would sit together at lunch on the days when their course met, and Dwayne would vent his anger at the financial system and the military-industrial complex while Kevin listened with great interest. Kevin was an unusually bright student and helped Dwayne with his assignments.

When Dwayne told Kevin about Bitcoin one day, Kevin, who was a hobby programmer in his spare time, was very interested in the technical details of the Bitcoin software. He began asking Dwayne many questions that Dwayne was unable to answer. Kevin resolved to research it himself.

A week later, Dwayne came to class early to review his textbook before the lecture. Just as he sat down and opened the book, Kevin rushed in, clearly excited.

"I built one!" he exclaimed.

"You built what?" Dwayne asked.

"A blockchain. It's really not that hard to do; it's just a network protocol."

He began telling Dwayne about his experiment, but much of what he said went completely over Dwayne's head. Dwayne remembered hearing about numerous other cryptocurrencies besides Bitcoin, and now that he realised Kevin could make one on his own, he understood why there were so many. He didn't have long to think about it as the class began soon after.

That day, one of their classmates gave a presentation about the use of loyalty programs. Using the example of frequent flyer miles, the student explained how rewards could be used to engineer demand for a product. As Dwayne listened, something clicked in his mind. He realised that frequent flyer miles or company-specific rewards were a kind of currency.

After class, Dwayne and Kevin went to get lunch as usual, and Dwayne started to ask Kevin technical questions about Bitcoin.

"How does the Bitcoin mining reward work?" he asked.

"Well, basically, miners provide a service to the network which secures the network, and they get a reward for it," Kevin replied.

"But could you issue that reward to someone else?"

"Sure, there's lots of currencies that build in a *developer tax*. A part of every block reward automatically goes to a development foundation that's responsible for developing and maintaining the network."

"But could you code a blockchain so that the block reward goes to anyone? Like, say, to reward people who spend money at certain businesses?" Kevin paused and thought about it for a moment.

"Well, I guess theoretically it would be possible."

Dwayne went on to describe an idea that had occurred to him during the lecture – a community currency with discounts and rewards for supporting local businesses. It could have inflation built in to encourage spending, but the new money created would be distributed to the small business owners and their customers. Small businesses could give discounts to customers for using the currency and earn rewards in exchange. Customers would be encouraged to support the local economy and would also earn rewards in the process.

They needed to come up with a subject for their final project anyway, and Kevin thought the idea sounded good. He was especially interested in the technical challenge of building it. They started to stay up late working on it together in the library on the nights when they had a class. Each night, the janitor had to ask them to leave at closing time.

After three weeks of intense work, they finished a prototype and presented it to the class. The presentation centred on how community currencies could promote economic growth within a community and how inflation, in the form of rewards distributed to users, acted as an incentive to support local businesses. Their professor was very impressed with their work and gave them a perfect score. They'd enjoyed the project so much that they decided to keep working on it.

Dwayne found many enthusiastic supporters for the idea at his Alcoholics Anonymous meeting, as well as at Veterans for Peace and the community garden. Kurt, who owned a welding shop, pledged that the shop would accept the currency as a form of payment. A small bakery owned by one of his neighbours in the community garden soon followed. Within several months, more than two dozen businesses had agreed to participate in the plan.

Kevin was thoroughly enjoying the coding aspect but realised it was too much work for one person. He'd been spending a lot of time online on forums for cryptocurrency enthusiasts and had heard about many crowdfunding successes. When he suggested setting up a crowdfund, Dwayne agreed.

Dwayne prepared a video about the idea, and Kevin helped him record it and uploaded it to YouTube. He then spread it on social media and cryptocurrency forums, and to their surprise, the video went viral. Within a month, they had raised enough money to rent an office and bring two more programmers on board. And so Dwayne and Kevin became the CEO and CTO of Peace Credits.

After six months of intense work, they were ready to launch the beta version of the new currency, complete with an app for tracking rewards and finding local businesses that accepted it. Their test users consisted of a few hundred community members. Apart from some minor glitches, which Kevin and his team fixed immediately, the launch went smoothly. After a few months, most of the issues were worked out, and the participating business owners all noted significant increases in their overall sales.

Once word got out, more businesses started contacting their office to enrol in the programme. With each business that joined the network, the more valuable peace credits became, and the keener customers were to earn them by spending at local businesses.

These earnings tipped the balance for many of the shoppers that used them. It gave local businesses an edge over corporate behemoths like Wal-Mart. Best of all, Dwayne felt that he was actually doing something to change the future for his children. The more people used peace credits, the less dependent they would all be on the war-addicted financial system. And the less they participated in that system, the less power it would have to drag his country into another ill-advised war.

One weekend, as he was dropping off his kids after spending the day with them, he asked Sandra if she'd like to come to a party. He was celebrating two years of being sober. She was surprised, but she agreed.

It was summer, and the party was at the community garden. Dwayne's friends from the garden, Alcoholics Anonymous, Veterans for Peace, and his colleagues from Peace Credits were all attending. There was a barbecue and organised games for the children. As the sun started to go down, the guests thanked Dwayne for hosting them and began to leave. Sandra collected the children and said goodbye as well.

"Sandra, I wanted to ask you something before you go," Dwayne said.

"Yes?" she replied.

"Would you... what do you think about dropping the kids with your parents this Friday and going to dinner with me?" he asked, a bit nervously. Sandra blushed and smiled.

"I'd love to, Dwayne."

Dwayne's heart leapt. He smiled, walked with them to the car and hugged the kids goodbye.

Dwayne had been sleeping much better. He realised it had been months since he'd seen the girl whose father he'd killed. That night, however, he woke up and saw her standing by his bedroom door. At first, he was filled with a sense of dread. Were the nightmares going to start again? Then he realised that something was different this time. The girl was calm and happy this time instead of screaming and crying. She looked at him calmly, smiled, and then disappeared.

∗ ∗ ∗

How Fiat Gets its Value

The interaction of supply and demand is very simple on the surface, but the implications can be very complex. Economist Warren Mosler once used a very simple and effective demonstration to explain the modern monetary system to an audience. He removed his business card holder from his pocket, removed several cards, and showed them to the audience. He then asked if anyone would like to buy one for $100. The audience laughed at the absurd suggestion.

Then he asked how their view would change if he told them there was only one exit from the auditorium, and his colleague was waiting at the door with a 9 mm handgun. His colleague would only allow them to exit the auditorium if they had one of his business cards.

Of course, this information, if true, would completely change the value of the business cards in the mind of the audience. Suddenly, $100 began to seem like a reasonable price.

This clever demonstration is an excellent way to understand how the value of fiat currency is generated. If people need it, it will have value. So really, it's very clever to invent a currency which only you can create and then require people to pay taxes with it under threat of violence. This guarantees demand for an asset on which you have a monopoly.

Once the use of a currency is established, it becomes normalised in the eyes of the people, and violence is no longer required to coerce them to use it. As its use becomes more common, it becomes even more valuable; there are even more sources of demand for that currency. The stronger the demand becomes, the more of the currency you can create without it going into hyperinflation. This is why the currencies of small countries go into hyperinflation much more easily than larger, internationally accepted currencies – there is simply less demand for them.

The position of the United States dollar as the world's reserve currency gives the US tremendous power over the world economy. The high demand for the dollar effectively acts as a limitless line of credit since demand for dollars is guaranteed no matter how many are created. The sources of this demand are many, including demand for products, commodities, and services, its use as a reserve currency for governments, and for paying taxes within the United States. But the single largest source of demand, and thus the biggest contributor to the power of the US dollar, is its relationship to oil.

Oil is the single most traded commodity in the world. And the only way to purchase the vast majority of that oil is with dollars. This creates an enormous, continuous worldwide demand for dollars.

Economists have long known about the strong relationship between dollars and oil. In fact, changes in dollar exchange rates are known to impact oil prices. But how did it get like this? If you want to buy wheat, you pay in the currency of the country where you buy the wheat. Not so with oil. No matter where you go, if you want to buy oil, you'll need dollars, with very few exceptions.

The only major oil-producing countries in the world that will sell oil for anything *other* than dollars are Iran and Venezuela. What else is special about these countries? Both of them are consistently in the crosshairs of American foreign policy. They are threatened and continuously battered with sanctions and coup attempts. Is this a coincidence?

Now, this is not to defend those regimes – surely, the governments of Venezuela and Iran are among the worst on the planet. Yet, there are many other corrupt, incompetent, and cruel regimes around the world that remain in the good graces of the international system. In addition to not playing along with the dollars-for-oil scheme, Iran and Venezuela have another major sin that might earn them the wrath of Uncle Sam – their central banks aren't part of the central bank club, centred in Switzerland – the Bank for International Settlements.

Other notable countries that are not part of this club are Russia, China, North Korea and Syria. Previous non-participants included Iraq and Libya. Are you starting to notice a pattern here? The international financial system seems to be saying, "It's either my way or the highway."

A number of scholars have supported the thesis that the purpose of the Iraq war was to protect the integrity of this system, sometimes called the "petrodollar". Saddam Hussein proposed selling oil for euros shortly before the US invasion, which led some to speculate that the move to abandon the petrodollar was part of the motivation for the invasion. Likewise, Libyan dictator Muammar Gaddafi also famously tried to begin trading oil for gold.

Gaddafi, like eGold and the Liberty Dollar, which were mentioned in the introduction, also had plans to establish a gold-backed currency and spread it throughout Africa in order to replace the fiat currency system. It's impossible to say if this was the real reason for the invasion, but there is certainly a clear motive. Publicly, of course, NATO's bombing of Libya was justified by the need to help establish human rights and democracy, but the decade long civil war that followed has ravaged the country's infrastructure, empowered extremist groups, and led to the deaths of thousands of innocent people. There doesn't seem to be as much funding for stabilising post-Gaddafi Libya as there was to remove Gaddafi, although it can hardly be said that the Libyan people's condition has improved as a result.

Of course, many mainstream academics still call the petrodollar thesis a conspiracy theory, and there are certainly those who take it too far. This is a complex and multi-faceted situation, so it might be an oversimplification to say that the wars and political conflicts associated with these countries are all about oil or maintaining the dominant position of the US dollar. There can be no doubt that maintaining the international financial system plays a major role, but how big a role is up for debate.

There is no question, however, that the nature of the currency system is very much linked to war.

The Origin of the Petrodollar

For more evidence of the link between fiat currency, the petrodollar, and war, we only need to look at the origin of the petrodollar system. Until 1971, the US dollar was officially backed by gold. After the Second World War, it was agreed at the Bretton Woods conference that the post-war monetary order would be based on the dollar, which would be backed by gold.

At the conference, John Maynard Keynes was a vocal advocate of the *Bancor*, a single world currency which he believed would facilitate world trade and reduce future conflicts. He was supported by a sizable, mainly British contingent. One of the reasons this plan was rejected was that no one could agree on who would control the Bancor. Ultimately, the American faction insisted that the future world order be based on the US dollar, very conveniently for themselves. Since the Americans had far more political clout, in the end, they got their way.

This arrangement did not last long. By the time US President John F. Kennedy was elected, there was already an active debate about devaluing the dollar in order to finance the US budget deficit.

Kennedy adamantly opposed such a move. On 23 July 1962, he spoke against breaking with the gold standard at a news conference:

The United States will not devalue its dollar, and the fact of the matter is the United States can balance its balance of payments any day it wants, if it wishes to withdraw its support of our defense expenditures overseas and our foreign aid.

Almost exactly three months later, Kennedy was assassinated. His successor, Lyndon Johnson, presided over an expansion in the money supply to finance the escalation of the Vietnam War. Of course, the Kennedy assassination has received more attention from conspiracy theorists than perhaps any other event in history. There is no conclusive evidence to support such conclusions, but those who challenge the financial system and war machine do seem to have a tendency to die rather violent deaths.

The supply of dollars was increased until the actual gold reserves were only backing a small percentage of the total dollars. Suspecting as much, France exchanged its dollars for gold in 1971, at which point US President Richard Nixon abandoned the gold standard completely. Before this, the number of dollars in circulation had increased to more than 20 times the total gold reserves, but at this point, the dollar lost all connection to any real asset, and an era of unlimited monetary debasement began.

Two years after this, turmoil in the Middle East began with the refusal of Saudi Arabia's King Faisal to sell oil. Two years later, King Faisal was assassinated by his nephew, who had just returned from America. The actual motive for the killing remains unknown, although there are many popular conspiracy theories that suggest some sinister plot. In any case, around this time, the states of the Persian Gulf all agreed to sell their oil for dollars and have not backed out of this agreement since.

Looking at the data, it's clear that the US was relatively balanced in terms of trade until the early 70s. After this, the values of imports began to exceed the value of exports. This is only possible by means of a massive expansion of debt.

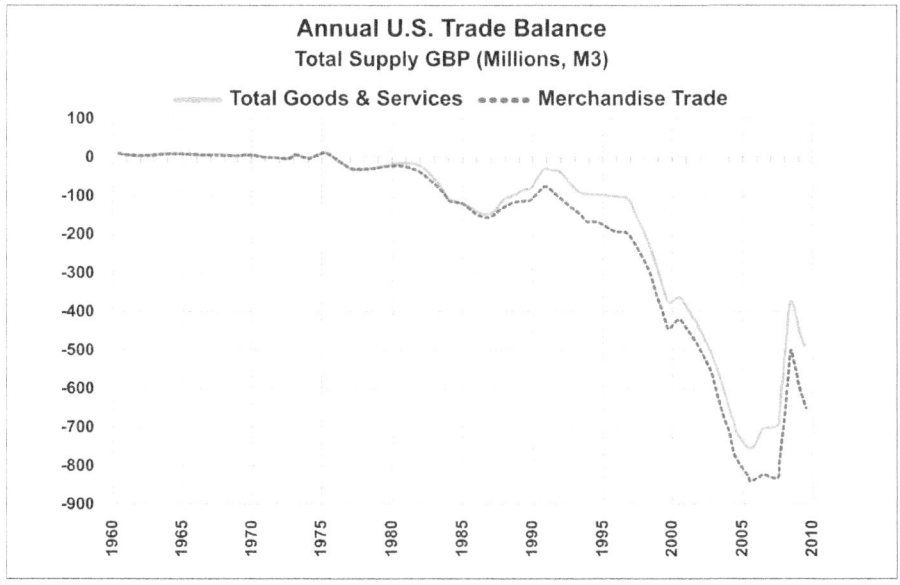

Annual U.S. Trade Balance
Total Supply GBP (Millions, M3)

Williams, John. Commentary Number 350, December Trade Deficit. February 11, 2011.

Perhaps, if the world could return to money that is grounded in reality and whose supply cannot be expanded on a whim, states would no longer be able to finance catastrophic and ill-advised wars like the invasions of Vietnam and Iraq. If wars had to be financed with real money rather than an endless supply of debt, perhaps politicians and taxpayers would be more careful about the use of violence to achieve their aims.

Fixing the System

This propensity for wars goes deeper than the ability to create money at will – it's also part of a longer cycle of booms, busts, and wars. Economists and scholars on both the left and right have written about these phenomena. Murray Rothbard identified it as beginning around the time of the industrial revolution:

Before the Industrial Revolution in approximately the late 18th century, there were no regularly recurring booms and depressions. There would be a sudden economic crisis whenever some king made war or confiscated the property of his subjects, but there was no sign of the peculiarly modern phenomena of general and fairly regular swings in business fortunes, of expansions and contractions.

Nikolai Kondratiev, a Soviet economist, was also famous for his exploration of these phenomena. Given the political context in which he was writing, it makes sense that he identified these cycles as belonging to the Western European breed of capitalism. Whatever the case may be, these cycles appear as expansions and contractions. The boom is usually accompanied by a rapid expansion of credit and lending and the bust by the disappearance of this fictitious wealth.

If we look at the real wealth transfer that takes place during these expansions and contractions, a clear trend of wealth concentrating in the hands of a smaller and smaller elite is visible, while the middle class comes under increasing pressure. This concentration of wealth can be overlooked at times when the economy is expanding, but when it contracts, the imbalance comes more starkly into contrast.

Economic historian Walter Scheidel discovered something startling about economic inequality. Throughout history, violence has a consistent effect of reducing economic inequality. We can't say that correlation is causation, but upsurges in violence consistently seem to accompany concentrations of large amounts of wealth in the hands of a few. And inflation appears to accelerate this process.

Inflation is not a natural condition. It depends on having money that is divorced from reality and can be created at will by corruptible human beings. And money that is divorced from reality is a major mechanism for transferring wealth from the poor to the rich. Adam Smith, regarded as the founder of modern economics, once said:

> *The problem with fiat currency is that it rewards the minority that can handle money but fools the majority that has worked and saved money.*

Why is this? Because with a steady rate of inflation, savings will lose value unless wisely invested. While there may be some exceptional and gifted individuals like Chaturi, most working people don't have time to understand the intricacies of investing. And so, the value of their savings goes down as the overall supply of money increases. John Maynard Keynes, the most influential economist of the 20th century, described it in similar terms:

By this means (fractional reserve banking), government may secretly and unobserved confiscate the wealth of the people, and not one man in a million will detect the theft.

But at some point, the theft becomes apparent, and things get violent.

This cycle of booms and busts would never be possible with hard money like gold, for example. Ironically, Alan Greenspan, the former chairman of the Fed, warned of this:

> *In the absence of the gold standard, there is no way to protect savings from confiscation through inflation [...] Deficit spending is simply a scheme for the "hidden" confiscation of wealth. Gold stands in the way of this insidious process. It stands as a protector of property rights.*

There's a very real danger that we are on course to repeat history. The world economy has made tremendous gains in the past century, and fewer people than ever are living in extreme poverty. But if these gains are not equitably distributed, it may all be for nought.

One of the core principles of physics, famously articulated by Sir Isaac Newton, is that "for every action, there is an equal and opposite reaction." You cannot simply steal the wealth of millions of people without consequences. Eventually, this whole charade has to come crashing down, as it always has in the past.

If we want to do something about war, finding a way to more evenly distribute wealth is a good place to start. The fractional reserve system has been a major engine for concentrating wealth in the hands of fewer and fewer individuals, and the break with the gold standard has supercharged this process. Consider the correlation between the end of the gold standard and income growth in the United States:

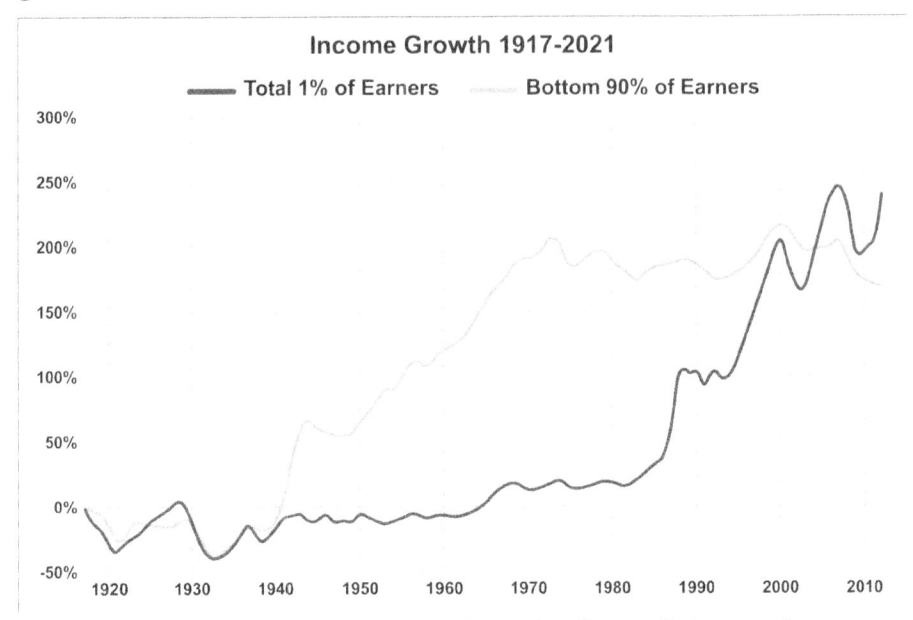

Income Growth 1917-2021

Source: Federal Reserve Economic Data, Institute for Fiscal Studies, Family Resources Survey

Of course, this is a complex process, and it's difficult to prove a causal link between the unlimited expansion of currency and inequality. However, it stands to reason that the wealthy are better able to weather inflation since they have more spare money to invest while working people are more likely to maintain savings in the form of cash.

Ending the reign of unlimited monetary expansion is certainly not a fix for human nature. We should have no utopian illusions that cryptocurrency is going to end war entirely. Moving towards wealth that retains its value, however, is certainly a step in the right direction.

Monopoly Money, and the Monopoly on Money

One of the most important concepts for understanding the power of cryptocurrency is the *network effect*. A network effect describes a phenomenon where, as a network grows, the more valuable individual parts of the network become.

A classic example is the telephone. If only two people have telephones, a telephone is not very useful, because they can only call each other. However, once ten people have telephones, there are many more possibilities for people to call each other. And once everyone has telephones – well, you can see how big the telecom industry is today.

With cryptocurrency, the situation is a bit different because the supply is limited. As the use of a currency increases, so does its utility, and thus demand for the currency. Combined with limited supply, this translates directly into price growth. We saw this with Dwayne's community currency. As more people joined the network, they could get discounts and earn rewards at more businesses by using the currency, and so the demand for the currency and its value increased in a virtuous cycle.

This same factor drives Bitcoin's growth, which is why some believe that Bitcoin will ultimately become the world reserve currency. But the fear is that if the price keeps going up, no one will want to spend their Bitcoin, and the economy could grind to a halt. Many prominent economists, including Nobel Prize winner Paul Krugman, have been outspoken opponents of Bitcoin for this reason.

There is surprisingly little agreement among economists as to the best way to run the economy. Austrian economists favour a limited money supply, while advocates of modern monetary theory argue for virtually unlimited expansion of the money supply. Essentially, these different schools of thought are based on fundamental beliefs about the world. It's not without good reason that mainstream economics is often referred to as *orthodox*. There is certainly a religious dimension to different schools of economic thought.

Adam Smith considered himself to be a moral philosopher first and foremost, and indeed, in the beginning, economics was concerned more with the wellbeing of society rather than simply maximising profits. With this moral dimension of economics in mind, the total dominance of one particular school of thought seems rather backward. Yet, central banks around the world all adhere to more or less the same economic philosophy.

Freedom of conscience, also known as freedom of religion, is considered an essential human right. At its core, monetary policy is very much an issue of belief. Most reasonable people today consider the notion of a single religious outlook being imposed upon an entire society by force as utterly abhorrent. Yet, in a way, imposing a particular notion of monetary policy on everyone is no less an imposition of beliefs.

Millions died in proxy conflicts during the cold war, and this war was in large part a conflict about competing visions of how the economy should be organised. The Soviet bloc believed in supply-side economics, while the West favoured letting the power of the market shape the economic order. When the Soviet Union fell and emigrants were finally given the freedom to leave, people were able to choose what type of economic system they wanted to live in.

What if people had simply been allowed to choose the type of economic system they wished to live in from the beginning, instead of fighting bloody and expensive wars to impose their vision upon the world? Why not simply let people live the way they want to live? Is "live and let live" really such a difficult motto to implement?

With cryptocurrency, for the first time in a very long while, we have the ability to choose what kind of monetary policy our wealth is subject to. Bitcoin, for example, is known for its volatility. Its exchange rate fluctuates wildly, but its value appreciates steadily. Fiat currency, on the other hand, is stable, but its value steadily depreciates.

For someone who values stability, fiat is naturally the better choice. And for someone who prefers long term appreciation and is not too concerned about stability, Bitcoin is clearly superior. Just as it is regarded as a fundamental right to have the freedom to practise the religion you want, why shouldn't we be free to live under whatever monetary policy we choose? Clearly, there is lots of money to be made by forcing people to use a currency that you control. With the rise of decentralised protocols, this incentive is completely removed.

Furthermore, the end of artificial currency monopolies will greatly reduce the ability of governments to run endless budget deficits. Eliminating the addiction to debt can make it much more difficult to conduct unnecessary and immoral wars.

It's understandable that the policymakers at Bretton Woods could not agree on a global currency. Being the custodian of the world reserve currency comes with massive potential for abuse. Indeed, there's quite a lot of evidence that giving this privilege to the United States was not the best decision. Until the invention of Bitcoin, there was never any possibility for a currency to exist outside the control of any and all governments.

Currency also has great symbolic power. US dollars carry symbols of American nationalism and are thus used to project American values. Currencies that are devoid of such symbols, like Bitcoin, can also promote a greater degree of unity. When the power to issue a currency is centred in a single nation or political bloc, there always exists the temptation for one country to hurt another's currency to boost its own.

With a currency that is not connected to any territory, political force, or nation, perhaps we can begin to see our common interests and work towards them. A new monetary paradigm and a more interconnected world that helps us to realise we're all in this together will surely be great progress towards a more peaceful and prosperous future.

Conclusion

In a time of deceit, telling the truth is a revolutionary act.
- GEORGE ORWELL

The Future of Money: Golden Age or Dystopia?

The ways that Bitcoin, cryptocurrency, and the associated technological revolution impacted the characters in every one of the stories in this book may be fictional, but they are also very real. Every story involves concrete, proven applications of this technology, and the experimental applications go well beyond what is described here.

Societies are ultimately composed of individuals, so if cryptocurrency can have such a profound effect on individuals, it is sure to have a powerful impact on global society. When it comes to understanding what the future holds, it can often be very helpful to look at the past. Many have compared the rise of Bitcoin and cryptocurrencies to the early days of the internet, but in fact, the impact of cryptocurrency is likely to be much bigger and more disruptive than what we have seen from the internet so far.

The internet has changed the way we communicate, the way we shop, our entertainment, the way we get around, and even the way we eat and sleep, but it has done little to change the fundamental power structures of our world. Amazon has challenged the retail industry, Uber has challenged the taxi industry, and WhatsApp and other messaging apps are disrupting the telecom industry, but until Bitcoin, nothing was able to challenge the power of those individuals and organisations that control the issuance of money.

The implications of such a shift in power cannot be explained using the internet alone. In fact, this shift may be more significant than the shifts brought about by the steam engine, the automobile, or the aeroplane. A number of observers have concluded that the past invention most comparable to cryptocurrency is actually the printing press.

Cryptocurrency vs the Printing Press

There are a surprising number of parallels between the impact of the printing press and the impact of Bitcoin. At the time the printing press was invented, there was a monopoly on a certain type of information, which was of the utmost importance to society at that time. Almost all production of books was controlled by the Catholic Church. A small elite decided which books were printed, and they only authorised Latin translations of the Bible, although most people couldn't understand Latin.

Priests claimed to be representing the interests of the people, but in reality, many of these elites were abusing their power in order to amass personal wealth at the expense of the people. Anyone who challenged this monopoly (by suggesting the earth revolves around the sun, for example) was shut down by force.

When the printing press was invented, the cost of books dropped dramatically. Printing shops across Europe began to print Bibles in local languages, and the hypocrisy of many priests was exposed. Furthermore, people were able to print and spread doctrines that the Church disapproved of, laying the foundation for future scientific revolutions.

Compare this to the situation with Bitcoin.

We have a small elite of bankers with a total monopoly on transactional information. Central bankers claimed to be protecting the interests of the people, regulating the money supply and interest rates in order to achieve maximum employment. A number of bankers, however, have been abusing their power to amass personal wealth at the expense of the people. Anyone who challenges this monopoly (by creating a private, gold-backed currency, for example) is shut down by force.

This comparison is at once very exciting and very troubling. It's exciting because the rise of the printing press brought forth an explosion of knowledge and ideas that culminated in the industrial revolution and a shift from feudalism to more representative forms of government. This was a sort of golden age where science, art, and culture flourished, which is now sometimes referred to as the Renaissance or the Age of Enlightenment.

A Monetary Renaissance

It might seem a bit unrealistic to expect cryptocurrencies to achieve similar results, but stop and think about it for a moment. What really enabled the progress that took place in the aftermath of the development of the printing press? For one, increased transfer of knowledge accelerated technological development, which resulted in more efficient economic production.

With better economic performance, people had more free time for activities other than struggling to survive. They could devote themselves to cultural pursuits like art, literature or music, or scientific pursuits like research, expeditions to remote areas to study plant and animal life, or developing new inventions. Ultimately, all of these opportunities relate to economic wellbeing.

So in order to determine whether cryptocurrency can truly have similar effects, we have to ask if it can have a similar economic effect. And it's very clear that it can.

The world is facing a crisis in the accumulation of wealth. There are just 2,153 billionaires in the world controlling more wealth than the poorest 4.6 billion people. In most of the world, this gap is growing.

Why is this a problem? Because the economy is driven by demand, and rich people don't consume as much as middle-class people.

If you give £1 million to 10 people, each one of them is likely to buy a house, a car, and do a fair bit of shopping and eating out. If you give £10 million to one person, they'll probably buy a bigger house, a nicer car, and go shopping and eating out at some more expensive shops and restaurants. But overall, one person with more money will generate much less economic activity than ten people with the same amount of money.

Even the most extravagant billionaire might purchase ten houses and 100 cars, but if you give a billion pounds to a thousand people instead, the number of jobs created will be vastly greater than those generated by the spending of a single billionaire.

Socialism and communism recognised this problem and sought to rectify it by seizing the wealth of the rich and abolishing private property, with horrific results. Communism is regarded by most historians as having caused more deaths than Nazi Germany, so although there are a few individuals who continue to advocate it, it should be fairly clear that this is not the answer.

The solution is not to confiscate the rightfully earned wealth of successful individuals, thus "punishing" success, as it were, but rather to amplify the earning potential of everyone else. Removing the power of banks to create money at will can go a long way towards accomplishing this goal.

Consider the AIG scandal of 2009. The American International Group, a US-based finance and insurance corporation, was hit hard by the financial crisis and received a bailout from the Fed. This was money created out of nothing. Even though the group posted over 60 billion dollars in losses that year, they went ahead with paying out bonuses to their executives. The total amount of these bonuses is unknown but is estimated to have exceeded one billion dollars.

There was outrage among the American public at the time, and the US Congress and Senate drafted laws to increase taxes on these bonuses. The laws were ultimately opposed by lobbyists for the financial sector and never passed.

This is just one prominent example of the abuse of the power of money creation, but many similar cases received less publicity, and many other examples are never discovered.

In the long run, preventing this kind of theft of value will make everyone better off. It's the world's poorest who are most severely hurt by our present currency system, and if they can escape the loss of value of their savings, they can make many more purchases, building the economy in the process. This could lead to an upsurge in economic growth that could drive innovation and social transformation, as did the advent of the printing press.

On the other hand, the prospect of a sort of New Reformation is also somewhat concerning. With the printing press, the people no longer needed to trust the Church for an officially sanctioned version of the truth and began to study and derive their own conclusions. This in itself is a wonderful thing, but unsurprisingly the Church was not keen to give up all of that power.

A horrifically bloody series of wars ensued, and it took decades of war before the Church finally acknowledged the right of states to exist outside its control. Is it possible that the move towards open money and financial freedom could trigger wars?

We can't discount that possibility. However, the view of bankers is softening toward Bitcoin. For example, J.P. Morgan CEO Jamie Dimon famously called Bitcoin a fraud in 2017, but by 2020 the same bank issued a report which stated

Bitcoin could compete more intensely with gold as an "alternative" currency over the coming years, given that millennials will become over time a more important component of investors' universe.

Perhaps this is an indication that the transition towards digital currencies need not be a zero-sum game, like the Church's monopoly on the truth. While banks will certainly lose a lot of power as a result of the cryptocurrency revolution, they also stand to profit from it by shifting their business models.

In July of 2020, US regulators announced that they had passed a law allowing commercial banks to hold Bitcoin deposits for their clients. As Bitcoin becomes more established, it's increasingly common to see Bitcoin used as collateral for loans. Just as email has not completely done away with the need of the post office, banks are likely to continue to play an important role in the future.

A key difference in this comparison is that the conflict with the Catholic Church during the Renaissance challenged the values of society on a fundamental level. The feudal system rested on the idea that all political authority must come from God and that the Pope was the sole representative of God on earth. During the Renaissance, this was challenged by the idea that individuals ought to have the right to choose what they believe and that societies should be able to choose how to govern themselves rather than deferring to the authority of the Pope.

No such change needs to happen in our time because most of the world already accepts these premises. The current structure of the global financial system actually runs very much *contrary* to the ideal of liberty. There is no need to overthrow these guiding principles; rather, the struggle is to restore the same rights that were established during the Renaissance.

John Locke famously summarised these rights as the right to "life, liberty, and property". Considering the matter carefully, it is clear that the present financial system violates all of these rights. The wealth of the people is stolen through inflation. Our freedom is compromised by a system that is based on debt rather than real wealth, and we all have to carry the burden of this debt whether we choose it or not. Finally, the maintenance of all this injustice and deception contributes to social strife and conflict, which, in some cases, costs people their lives.

So this revolution is not about overturning the values of a society. Rather, it's about upholding them. This is cause for hope that the transition we are going through need not result in violence. In the case of the Catholic Church, millions of people earnestly believed that their salvation depended on obedience to the Church. It's unlikely that the international banking system will enjoy this kind of support.

Therein lies part of the motivation for this book. If we can understand that our financial system has become riddled with deception and theft, then we can withdraw our support from the individuals and institutions engaged in destructive and immoral practices. It is the spread of knowledge and understanding that can prevent the kind of misunderstandings that lead to conflict. If we understand that a more open and transparent financial system will be beneficial to all of us, then the transition can go much more smoothly.

The Power of Truth

At its core, Bitcoin is a radical truth-telling technology. Although it doesn't always get the attention it deserves in economic analysis, truth is actually essential to the health of an economy as well as many other aspects of our lives.

It's the ability to know that someone is truthful that enables trust, and trust is the basis of any healthy relationship. Good relationships are fundamental to the generation of value in our lives and in the world. Business partners must trust each other in order to succeed in a venture. Students must trust that teachers are conveying accurate information in order to learn. Trust is even the foundation of love – to fall in love, you must trust that your partner will not break your heart. There are so many ways in which trust builds value in our lives; it's hard to believe that our world is governed by a financial system that is so rife with violations of trust.

The essential innovation of Bitcoin is that it enables transactions between two parties without the need for trust, but this trustlessness can be the foundation of a system that actually *builds* trust. Transparency and honesty can be more than just a desirable quality; transparency in finance can now become the norm.

Some view cryptocurrency as a lifeboat that can be used to escape the sinking ship of the global economy, but it's really much more than that. For Emily and Noah, it enabled them to leverage their kindness and goodwill to buy a home in the midst of a financial crisis. For Amadou, it helped him combat the scourge of corruption in his homeland. In the case of Adriana, it was a catalyst for finding new ways to fight crime in an increasingly globalised world. For Yuri, it was a job opportunity and a way to put underutilised resources to good use. For Farhan, it provided a lifeline for exposing an oppressive regime. For Chaturi, it opened doors of opportunity for her to improve her own life and the life of her community. And for Dwayne, it was a means of peaceful dissent and absolution.

All of these stories were made possible by the ability of a decentralised, peer-to-peer network to preserve the authenticity of information - to preserve and convey the truth. This is a great power and a great responsibility. It takes a leap of faith to make the transition from the old to the new, but fortune favours the bold. There is no turning back, so we must embrace the change that is upon us. If we do, the future of money, and our world, is in our hands.

References

Assange, Julian, et al. *Cypherpunks: Freedom and the Future of the internet.* New York: OR Books, 2016.

Back, Adam. *Hashcash- A Denial of Service Counter-Measure.* 2002. http://www.hashcash.org/papers/hashcash.pdf

Bendiksen, Christopher & Gibbons, Samuel. (2019) The Bitcoin Mining Network - Trends, Composition, Average Creation Cost, Electricity Consumption & Sources. CoinShares Research

BIS Member Banks. Bank for International Settlements, 2019. https://www.bis.org/about/member_cb.htm

Cox, Jason. Koebler, Joseph (2019). "Twitter Has Started Researching Whether White Supremacists Belong on Twitter". *Vice.* https://www.vice.com/en_us/article/ywy5nx/twitter-researching-white-supremacism-nationalism-ban-deplatform

Goodwin, Jonathan. (2019) A Free Money Miracle? Mises Daily Articles. https://mises.org/library/free-money-miracle

Gokay, Bulent. "The beginning of the end of the petrodollar: What connects Iraq to Iran." *Alternatives: Turkish Journal of International Relations* 4.4 (2005).

Hinchey, Michael G., Roy Sterritt, and Chris Rouff. "Swarms and swarm intelligence." *Computer* 40, no. 4 (2007): 111-113.

Huntington, H. G. (1986). The US dollar and the world oil market. *Energy policy*, *14*(4), 299-306.

International Monetary Fund (IMF). Global Financial Stability Reports, 2019. https://www.imf.org/en/Publications/GFSR/Issues/2019/10/01/global-financial-stability-report-october-2019

Irwin, Neil. *The Alchemists: Three Central Bankers and a World on Fire*. New York: The Penguin Press, 2013.

Karombo, Tawanda. (2019) Zimbabwe banned the US dollar from being used so local bitcoin demand is soaring again. Quartz Africa. https://qz.com/africa/1662753/bitcoin-crypto-soar-in-zimbabwe-again-after-us-dollar-ban/

Kelly, Jackson. (2017) Criticisms of Proof of Stake. https://sjkelleyjrblog.wordpress.com/2017/09/16/criticisms-of-proof-of-stake/

Kennedy, John F. (1962) News Conference 39, July 23, 1962. John F. Kennedy Presidential Library and Museum. https://www.jfklibrary.org/archives/other-resources/john-f-kennedy-press-conferences/news-conference-39

Kim, Jongchul. "How modern banking originated: The London goldsmith-bankers' institutionalisation of trust." *Business History* 53.6 (2011): 939-959.

Kshetri, Nir. Chinese internet users turn to the blockchain to fight against government censorship. *The Conversation*. (February, 2019) https://theconversation.com/chinese-internet-users-turn-to-the-blockchain-to-fight-against-government-censorship-111795

Levy, Steven. *Crypto: How the Code Rebels Beat the Government-- Saving Privacy in the Digital Age*. New York: Penguin Books, 2002.

New York Sun. "Beyond Bernard Von NotHaus." The New York Sun Editorial. December 2, 2014. https://www.nysun.com/editorials/beyond-bernard-von-nothaus/88958/

Nicholls, Anthony J. *Weimar and the Rise of Hitler*. New York: St. Martin's Press, 2000.

Orcutt, Mike. (2019) China says its digital currency will have controllable anonymity— but who will control it? MIT Technology Review. https://www.technologyreview.com/f/614711/china-says-its-digital-currency-will-have-controllable-anonymitybut-who-will-control-it/

Paul, Helen. (2013) *The South Sea Bubble: An Economic History of its Origins and Consequences*

Pixley, J. (2018). Vietnam War, Dollar Float and Nixon. In *Central Banks, Democratic States and Financial Power* (pp. 213-255). Cambridge: Cambridge University Press.

Rothbard: *The Austrian Theory of the Trade Cycle and Other Essays*, The Mises Institute,1983.

Savage, Michael. (2019). *Millennial housing crisis engulfs Britain.* The Guardian. https://www.theguardian.com/society/2018/apr/28/proportion-home-owners-halves-millennials

Scheidel, Walter. *The Great Leveler : Violence and the History of Inequality from the Stone Age to the Twenty-First Century.* Princeton, New Jersey: Princeton University Press, 2017.

Schwartz, Oscar. (2018) Are Google and Facebook Really Suppressing Conservative Politics?
The Guardian. https://www.theguardian.com/technology/2018/dec/04/google-facebook-anti-conservative-bias-claims

Shipley, Tyler (March 2007). "Currency Wars: Oil, Iraq, and the Future of Us Hegemony". *Studies in Political Economy.*

Shor, Francis. "War in the era of declining US global hegemony." *Journal of Critical Globalisation Studies* 2 (2010):

Taleb, Nassim N. The black swan: the impact of the highly improbable. New York: Random House, 2007.

Tullock, Gordon. "Paper Money-A Cycle in Cathay." *The Economic History Review* 9, no. 3 (1957): 393-407.

Warner, Bernhard. "AI Remains a Disruptive Force in Finance—Even for Fintechs" Fortune. October 10, 2019. https://fortune.com/2019/10/10/artificial-intelligence-disruptive-force-finance-even-for-fintechs/

Wynbrandt, James (2010). *A Brief History of Saudi Arabia*. Infobase Publishing. p. 236

Zetter, Kim. "Bullion and Bandits: The Improbable Rise and Fall of E-Gold." Wired. Conde Nast, March 21, 2018. https://www.wired.com/2009/06/e-gold/.

Home prices graph sources: St. Louis Fed, UK Land Registry, OECD Data, Office for National Statistics

https://www.reuters.com/article/us-global-migrants-un/migrants-losing-25-billion-per-year-through-remittance-fees-un-idUSKCN1NP2BA

Russell
https://techcrunch.com/2019/01/21/facebook-airbus-solar-drones-internet-program/

Cimpanu
https://www.zdnet.com/article/moscows-blockchain-voting-system-cracked-a-month-before-election/

Merkle, Ortrun. Corruption and Migration: what is the connection? http://nvvn.nl/corruption-and-migration-what-is-the-connection/

McGath, Thomas. M-PESA: how Kenya revolutionized mobile payments https://mag.n26.com/m-pesa-how-kenya-revolutionized-mobile-payments-56786bc09ef

Anser, M.K., Yousaf, Z., Nassani, A.A. *et al.* (2020) Dynamic linkages between poverty, inequality, crime, and social expenditures in a panel of 16 countries: two-step GMM estimates. *Economic Structures* 9, 43. https://doi.org/10.1186/s40008-020-00220-6

About the Author

Mihir Magudia is passionate about disruptive technologies and has an optimistic hope that they can make the world a better place. He wrote this book in 2020 at a moment when the whole world had the opportunity to consider a radically different future. He was born and raised in Hertfordshire in the United Kingdom.